·100 CATASTROPHIC·
DISASTERS

·100 CATASTROPHIC·
DISASTERS

NIGEL CAWTHORNE

Capella

This edition published in 2006 by Arcturus Publishing Limited
26/27 Bickels Yard, 151–153 Bermondsey Street,
London SE1 3HA

In Canada published for Indigo Books
468 King St W,
Suite 500,
Toronto,
Ontario M5V 1L8

ISBN-13: 978-1-84193-169-2
ISBN-10: 1-84193-169-1

Printed in China

Contents

Earthquakes

Tsunami

Floods

Hurricanes

Air disasters

Shipwrecks

Community Disasters

Volcanoes

Sporting Disasters

Space Disasters

Avalanches

Train Crashes

Fires

Earthquakes

Imperial Chinese records provide information on the number of casualties in the 1556 earthquake

Shensi, China 1556

The earthquake centred on Hausien in the Shensi (or Shaanxi) province of China on the night of 23 January 1556 is thought to be the worse natural disaster in recorded history in terms of lives lost. Estimated to be of a magnitude of 8.0 to 8.3 on the Richter scale, it devastated ninety-eight counties and eight provinces of Central China.

The destruction spanned an area of five hundred square miles, and in some counties the average death toll was sixty per cent of the population. A total of 830,000 people lost their lives according to imperial records. This was because many lived in poorly constructed houses whose roofs collapsed or artificial caves dug in cliffs in the plateau of the loess, or soft clay, formed over millions of years by silt blown there from the Gobi Desert 200 miles to the north-west.

The earthquake also struck at night when most people were indoors, ensuring a higher death toll. Survivors of the initial quakes also found themselves victims of subsequent fires, landslides and floods caused, in part, by the quake. The tremor was so big that people felt it in over half of China.

Another earthquake of magnitude 8.6 on the Richter scale hit the Chinese province of Kansu to the north-west on 16 December 1920 killing some 180,000 people directly. A further 20,000 were thought to have died due to lack of shelter during the bitter winter that followed.

An even more catastrophic earthquake is thought to have occurred in the same area in the mid-1950s. Some estimates of the death toll put it even higher than the Ming dynasty's 1556 record-holder. Up to a million people may have perished, but the Communist government which came to power in 1949 never confirmed the disaster or released any details of what happened.

China is particularly susceptible to earthquakes because it sits on the so-called "ring of fire" – the band of volcanic activity that rings the Pacific – and the northward movement of the Indian plate that collides with the Asian plate in the vicinity of the Himalayas. Seismology – the study of earthquakes – is thought to have originated in China.

Antioch, Turkey
AD 526

In the sixth century, Antioch – now Antakya in Turkey – was a bustling trading centre with a long history. Founded by the Greeks in 300 BC, it had become the capital of the Seleucid Kingdom, then the provincial capital of Syria under the Roman Empire. When the imperial capital was moved eastwards from Rome to Constantinople, Antioch's importance as a commercial city grew. It had paved streets lit by oil lights, theatres, amphitheatres and public baths, all ringed by a massive stone wall.

Antioch was also one of the cradles of Christianity, the secure base for Paul's mission to the Gentiles. And the Emperor Constantine had built the Great Church with its golden-dome there.

On 29 May 526, the city was busier than usual. Thousands of Christians had

> "fire fell down from heaven like rain… as if it had received a commandment from God that every living thing should be burned."

flocked there for the feast of Ascension, the following day. Soon after 6 pm, when people had gone indoors at dusk, the earthquake struck without warning. Whole buildings collapsed in an instant, crushing those inside. An eerie silence followed. Then came the aftershocks, followed by a swift-moving fire. The flames blocked any route of escape. Survivors were burnt to death as they fled. Those trapped under the rubble were consumed where they lay or suffocated.

One of the few survivors, John Malalas, said that the "fire fell down from heaven like rain… Sparks of fire filled the air and burned like lightning. Except for the soil, the fire surrounded everything in the city, as if it had received a commandment from God that every living thing should be burned."

According to Malalas: "Not a single dwelling, nor house of any sort, no church, nor monastery, nor any other holy place was left intact." Miraculously, "after everything else had fallen by the wrath of God", the Great Church of Constantine "remained standing for five days after the punishment. But suddenly even it caught on fire and collapsed to the ground."

It is estimated that between 250,000 and 300,000 people were killed in the initial shock and fire, or perished later among the rubble. Hordes of other thieves descended on the ruins, stripping the corpses of their clothes and jewellery, and tearing gold inlays and precious ornaments from the buildings. Survivors stumbling from the devastated city were attacked by bandits who stole their valuables and murdered anyone who resisted. One notorious thief was a man called Thomas who stationed his slaves at the city gates and amassed a fortune. But soon after he died and his plunder was dispersed. This was seen as an example of divine retribution.

Other miraculous tales circulated. Malalas said that pregnant women who had been trapped under the rubble for as long as three weeks came out unscathed, bringing their healthy babies with them. Other survivors said that they saw a cross hanging in the sky for more than an hour, three days after the earthquake. They fell on their knees and gave thanks. But no one could explain why God would want to destroy such a beautiful city.

"The splendour of the city, its good climate and the beauty of its churches were such that those strangers who had seen it before and came there afterwards exclaimed: 'So utterly has this great refuge, this peace harbour of the world, been desolated,'" wrote Malalas. "Antioch the Great collapsed by the wrath of God."

In fact, Antioch had been struck by an earthquake nine times. In AD 115 the Roman Emperor Trajan and the future Emperor Hadrian barely escaped with their lives, Trajan having to crawl through a window to get out of the collapsed building he was in. On that occasion it was said that the growing Christian minority in the city had offended the gods. The Bishop of Antioch, Ignatius, was taken in chains to Rome where he was tried, convicted and thrown to the wild animals in the Colosseum.

This time the earthquake was blamed on Justin I. A spate of quakes in the area had started soon after he came to the Byzantine throne in 518. When Justin heard of the destruction of Antioch, he "took off his crown and the purple robe, mourned for a long time and wept," according to Malalas. Troops were sent to search for survivors. When Justinian succeeded Justin in 527, he sent money to have the city rebuild. But a new earthquake hit Antioch in November 528, killing another five thousand. Survivors began to move away out of the area, but Justinian was determined to have the city rebuilt once again, sent more money and gave all those who stayed behind a three-year tax break. He also decided to placate God by changing the name of the city from Antiochus to Theopolis, which means "City of God". It did no good. In 540, the city was sacked by the Persians. Two years later the survivors were ravaged by the plague. The city was captured again by the Persians in 611 and shrank to a small town under the Arab caliphate, which took over the city in 637.

Tangshan, China 1976

Tangshan, a city of a million people, lies in the coal-mining region of China some hundred miles south-east of Peking, and is a centre for electricity generation. At 3.45 am on 29 July 1976, flashing multi-coloured lights visible over two hundred miles away appeared over the city. In twenty-three seconds, the heart of the city, some twenty square miles of buildings, was completely destroyed by an earthquake registering some 7.8 to 8.2 in the Richter scale.

Some people were thrown six foot in the air. Hiroshi Toyota, a technician from Japan, awoke to find that his bed had plunged through three floors of his hotel.

Ho Shu-sen, a senior police officer, was woken by his wife moments before the earthquake hit.

"I saw a quick flash of greenish-blue light in the sky."

"I saw a quick flash of greenish-blue light in the sky," he said, "and heard a strange sound from under the ground like the noise of a freight train. The floor began jerking up and down. I jumped out of the window, but the earth shook back and forth and threw me to the ground. My house collapsed. For two or three minutes there was no sound. Then I heard people crying everywhere in the darkness in the ruins of their homes."

In some places cracks several feet wide had appeared in the earth. Fences had been knocked four-and-a-half feet out of line and railway tracks buckled. And thousands of sinkholes had opened up like so many bomb craters.

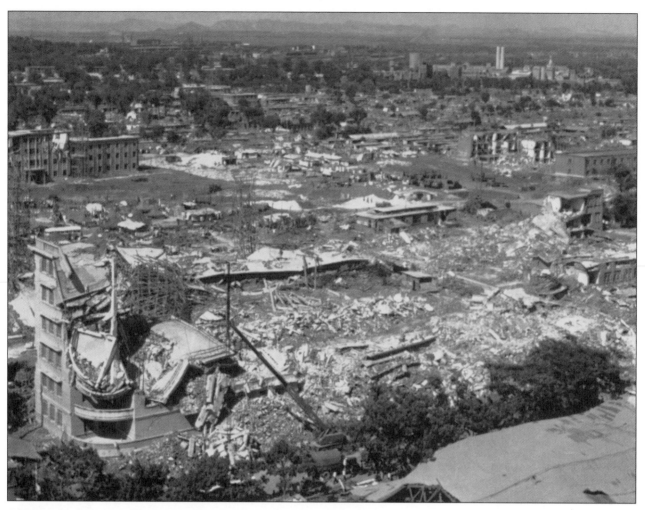

Aftermath: the city of Tangshan lies in ruins after the earthquake

Over sixty miles away at Tientsin, the former prime minister of Australia Gough Whitlam and his wife fled from the seventh floor of the Friendship Guest House, which they said "literally split down the middle" with a one-foot gap separating the two parts.

"Outside people were digging under the rubble," said Mrs Whitlam. "Whole facades of buildings had come down."

New Yorkers Samuel and Beatrice Steinberg, on a tour of China organised by his union, were also staying there. They clung together in the darkness, convinced they were going to die. Leaving behind all their luggage, they were bussed out of the city for fear of after shocks. But while some of the older buildings collapsed, the newer ones survived.

In Peking a hundred people were killed when older structures collapsed and six million fled their homes and camped out in the torrential rain storm that followed the initial shock of the earthquake.

In the next forty-eight hours, 125 aftershocks were recorded in north-east China. The strongest occurred sixteen hours after the tremor that destroyed Tangshan. In all, it is estimated that ninety-five per cent of Tangshan's civil buildings and eighty per cent of its industrial plants suffered severe damage. And of the giant smokestacks – ironically emblazoned with the Maoist slogan "Prepare for war and natural disaster" – only one was left standing.

The Communist media were loathe to report such a disaster, particularly as Chinese scientists claimed that they could predict earthquakes from the strange behaviour of animals and the sudden change in the level and temperature of water in wells. Indeed, just such a forecast in February 1975 had saved thousands of lives in Liaoning Province. But there was no warning at Tangshan.

> "… I heard people crying everywhere in the darkness in the ruins of their homes."

The heart of the city of Tangshan was destroyed in just 23 seconds

"In the interests of the people of the neighbourhood... he did not hesitate to sacrifice his children."

By 5 pm, military planes were dropping food, water, medical supplies and clothing into the city. The following day a huge column of aid workers arrived from Peking and the injured were taken in convoys back to hospitals in the city. The army moved in to seal up the corpses in plastic body bags, to prevent an epidemic, and bury them in mass graves outside the city. Some 30,000 medical personnel, 30,000 construction workers and 100,000 troops were involved in the rescue operation.

Communist leader Mao Tse-tung issued the party directive that all people should "plunge into the anti-quake fight with a firm and indomitable hand... guided by Chairman Mao's revolutionary line". According to the *People's Daily*, Che Cheng-min answered the call. Apparently he dragged himself from the wreck of his home and was about to go to the rescue of his thirteen-year-old

daughter and his sixteen-year-old son, when he heard the cries of Chiu Kuang-yu, the secretary of the neighbourhood Communist Party committee. Naturally, he abandoned his children and went to the aid of the party official. "When he returned home, Che Cheng-min found his two children dead," said the newspaper. "But he felt neither remorse nor grief. In the interests of the people of the neighbourhood and the majority interest, he did not hesitate to sacrifice his children."

Ho Shu-shen, the Tangshan police captain, managed to escape from his house with his sixteen-year-old son just before it collapsed. They managed to dig out Ho's wife and two other sons, but his fourteen-year-old daughter was dead. Then, with his sons, he managed to rescue nineteen neighbours. With these, he organised a rescue team. Then he set up a makeshift police station and, bare-foot,

in his underwear and brandishing a pistol, he managed to arrest seventy looters over the next couple of days.

One of the reasons the Chinese authorities wanted to keep quiet about the Tangshan disaster was that, according to Chinese superstition, an earthquake is supposed to herald a major political upheaval, such as the end of a dynasty. Six weeks after the Tangshan earthquake, Mao Tse-tung died.

Initially unofficial estimates put the death toll at between 750,000 and a million. But three years later the official figure of 242,000 was published. Another 164,000 were thought to be seriously injured − among them 1,700 paraplegics − and some 2,600 children were orphaned. The reason for the high death toll was that the epicentre was directly under the city and the earthquake occurred at night, when most people were indoors.

After some wrangling about whether they should rebuild on an earthquake-prone site, the city was rebuilt in 1979.

Messina, Italy 1908

At 5.20 am on the rainy morning of 28 December 1908, the Sicilian port of Messina was rocked by the first of three earth tremors that destroyed ninety per cent of its buildings and killed the majority of its population of 100,000 in their sleep. One of the survivors, Rosina Calabresi, told a newspaper reporter simply: "Messina non esiste più" − "Messina is no more."

Nobody is sure how many died. The epicentre of the earthquake, measuring 7.5 on the Richter scale, was under the Straits of Messina that separate Sicily

A few lucky survivors wander through the ruins of Messina

from the Italian mainland. So just as the survivors were clambering out from under the rubble, they were hit by a twenty-six-foot tsunami that swept them out to sea. Others were burnt to death when a ruptured gas main set the town on fire. Contemporary estimates put the death toll as high as 90,000 in Messina itself and 40,000 in the mainland port of Reggio di Calabria. Another 27,000 were thought to have died in the towns and villages along the straits. Later the official figure was put at 120,000.

Rosina Calabresi and her husband, along with their son Francisco, his wife and their two children, managed to escape into the rain.

"The earth groaned as it rocked from side to side as if it were in pain," said Francisco. "Though the house fell down about us we were not hurt. The door to the street was jammed and would not open. I found a small hole in the wall near it and managed to crawl out through it and help the others out."

They spent two days and nights in the open until two Russian sailors came to their rescue. They gave the family food and clothing and safe passage on their warship to the port of Ostia.

The Calabresis were saved by the fact they lived in a small, well-built house. The houses of the rich, particularly, were deathtraps. Messina's impressive palaces and public buildings had thin high walls made of pebbles bound together with inferior cement, even though the city had been severely damaged by an earthquake in 1783. This turned to dust at the

> **"Messina non esiste più" – "Messina is no more."**

Many had to salvage what belongings they could and move on

first tremor. The cathedral, the army barracks, the military hospital and the hotels all fell down, engulfing the buildings around them.

London shipbroker Constantine Doresa was staying at the Trinscria Hotel. After being jolted awake, he "clutched at the sides of the bed, which seemed to be falling through space... Then came a series of crashes, the roof falling around me. I was smothered in brick and plaster... I felt for matches, struck a light and was horrified to find my bed on the side of an abyss."

With the aid of knotted sheets, Doresa and his travelling companion managed to lower themselves to safety, rescuing a Swedish couple on the way. They later returned to the hotel with the crew of a Welsh steamer, some Russian sailors and ladders and ropes to rescue other guests.

The captain of a Russian cruiser pulled two babies from the rubble unharmed.

"They were laughing and playing with the buttons on their clothes," he wrote.

Accounts tell of half-naked survivors stumbling injured through the rubble of the streets.

"The spectacle that greets the eye here is beyond the imagination of Jules Verne," wrote the Marquis di Ruvolito.

Looters set about robbing the shops and warehouses, and stripping the corpses of their valuables. Even law-abiding survivors were forced to forage for food, water and clothing in the cold.

The Russian sailors did what they could to prevent looting, and British and Italian ships rushed to the port to lend aid. The American Relief Committee in Rome hired the German liner *Bayern* to send supplies. Relief poured in from all over Italy, Europe and the US. And two days after the disaster, King Victor Emanuel and Queen Elena of Italy turned up to lend a hand.

> ### "The spectacle is beyond the imagination of Jules Verne."

Messina was rebuilt with low, concrete-reinforced buildings in the wake of the earthquake

The rescue operation in Messina discovered very few people alive under the rubble

After the 1908 earthquake new building regulations were brought in and Messina was rebuilt with wide streets and low, reinforced-concrete buildings. The cathedral and the Church of Annunciata dei Catalani, of Byzantine origin and rebuilt by the Normans in the twelfth century, were restored and the National Museum houses works of art saved from the earthquake.

Armenia 1988

At 11.41am on 7 December 1988, an earth-quake measuring 6.9 on the Richter scale hit Armenia, a densely populated republic of the former Soviet Union which lay along the border with Turkey. Four minutes later an aftershock of magnitude 5.8 hit.

The town of Spitak was virtually "erased from the face of the earth," as one reporter put it. In nearby Kirovakan, a city of 170,000, nearly every building of any size had collapsed. High-rise apartment blocks made of prefabricated concrete slabs had become instant tombs for their inhabitants.

At Leninakan thirty miles to the west, the ceiling of a classroom at Elemental School Nine on Gorky Street collapsed on the heads of fifty children, while 250 people were trapped inside a computer centre. The walls of the ancient cathedral collapsed, though the dome was left intact and the Armenian Seismic Institute was destroyed, along with all its instruments. In all, some 4,000 square miles were devastated.

Some people died by chance. A factory manager went home during a break and was buried along with his children. But fate was kinder to others. A woman was buried beneath the wreckage of her office, leaving only her hand protruding.

15,000 men, women and children were found alive beneath the rubble of Kirovakan

Her son spotted a familiar wedding ring and dug her out.

Muffled cries for help came filtering up through the devastation. Others were not so lucky. As volunteers cleared the rubble, lines of corpses were laid along the streets for identification and burial, while survivors wrapped in coats and blankets warmed themselves by bonfires.

Bringing relief to the stricken cities was almost impossible. Armenia is a mountainous country. The roads were blocked by landslides and the railway line to the neighbouring republic of Georgia was cut. It was estimated that, with every hour's delay, another twenty people would be dead. And just as an airlift got underway, a December fog closed in on the airport at Yerevan, the capital of Armenia. A Soviet transport coming into land crashed killing all seventy-nine on board. A second plane,

bringing medical supplies from Yugoslavia, also crashed, killing its crew.

Eventually the Soviet Army arrived with 6,500 troops and heavy bulldozers. Twenty-five brigades of military doctors were brought in, while the inhabitants of Moscow queued up to donate blood, blankets and clothing.

For the first time since World War II, the Soviets accepted American aid. Eight US government transports flew in earthmoving equipment and relief supplies. These were followed by twelve more supplied by charities and the US alone spent $14.5 million on relief.

In all sixty-seven nations came to Armenia's aid. The British brought sensitive listening devices and fibre-optic probes to hunt for survivors under the rubble. The French brought sniffer dogs. West Germany sent sixteen cranes; Japan $9 million, while the Italians erected prefabricated homes.

lines of corpses were laid along the streets

Armenia is famous for its stone – but the natural commodity became a killer on 7 December

Maharastra State, India 1993

The relief workers soon found themselves in a race against time. The temperature plummeted and the rubble was soaked with freezing rain. Victims pried alive from the rubble died on the way to hospital. At Elementary School Nine, a volunteer had plucked forty-eight corpses from under the collapsed ceiling – then, miraculously, found one child alive.

Soon the muffed cries stopped. But a week after the earthquake twenty more survivors were dug out of the wreckage of Leninakan. One more was found in Spitak. But that was it. Some 15,000 victims had been rescued from the rubble and 25,000 dead bodies were found. No one is sure how many died, but the economic loss was estimated at $14.2 billion.

Much of India is in an earthquake zone and many lists of the world's most destructive earthquakes include an earthquake in Calcutta in 1737 which is said to have to have killed 300,000 people. However, the population of Calcutta at the time was of the order of 3,000. Even a century later the population had only grown to 30,000. And the number of burials in St Anne's Church, Calcutta, was only ten per cent higher in 1737 than in the preceding and following decades. However, the latest research shows that there was a hugely destructive cyclone around that time.

More recently, an earthquake measuring 6.3 on the Richter scale hit the Latur-Osmanabad area of the India state of Maharashtra at 3.56 am on the morning of 30 September 1993. It lasted less than fifty seconds and damaged fifty villages in a fifty-mile radius. Sixteen were levelled completely. The death toll estimate by the Maharastra government was around 7,600, and about 15,000 were injured in the quake. However, other sources put the death toll as high as 22,000 or even 30,000. Many of the people killed were asleep in badly-constructed stone houses that collapsed on top of them.

India is particularly susceptible to earthquakes because the movement of the Earth's tectonic plates is forcing the subcontinent northwards into the bulk of Asia. The Indian and the Asian plates meet deep under the Himalayas. The country is also densely populated, a fact that contributes to the high casualty figures after any natural disaster. On 16 June 1819, an earthquake in the west of the country at Kutch killed 1,500 and on 12 June 1897 another 1,000 perished to the east in Assam. And some 60,000 died on 31 May 1935 at Quetta in Baluchistan after an earthquake that measured 7.5 on the Richter scale.

Sixteen villages were completely levelled by the 1993 earthquake in India's Maharastra State

Guatemala 1976

Guatemala's location in Central America places it in a highly geologically unstable region. The small country has nine volcanoes, one of which, Fuego, has erupted sixty times since 1524, making it the most active volcano in Central America. Its 1974 eruption was the most voluminous in recent history. Pacaya has erupted twenty-three times since 1565 and has been erupting pretty much constantly since 1965. While Santa Mariá produced the second largest eruption of the twentieth century in 1902, blasting out 1.3 cubic miles of ejecta.

The country is also susceptible to earthquakes. On the night of 8 April 1902, a thirty- to forty-second quake left 20,000 dead in Quetzaltenango. The death toll from the initial tremor was compounded by a rainstorm and the city's loss of electrical power and lighting. People fleeing ran down the

58,000 houses were destroyed in Guatemala City

The rural communities of Guatemala were ill-equipped to cope with disaster on such a scale

streets unable to see where they were going. They died when walls fell on them. Others drowned in the torrents caused by the downpour, and after-shocks, which continued for the next three days, hampered rescue work.

Rumblings continued. In the 1950s, there were some five hundred small quakes a year. These dropped off to around 250 a year in the 1960s and 1970s. Pressure was building up in the crust. Then on 4 February 1976, a 30-second shock reaching 7.5 on the Richter scale was felt from Costa Rica to Mexico City. A slippage of five feet had taken place on the fault line that passes through Guatemala. Landslides buried villages. Some 22,778 people died and some 80,000 were injured. The slippage cut houses in two and severed road, railway lines and bridges, making it almost impossible to get relief to the needy as the country had few helicopters.

Forty miles away in San Pedro Sacatépequez, an Indian entrepreneur named Cleto Monroy felt the shock, grabbed his two children and ran out of his house before its walls collapsed.

"I thought it was only my own house that had fallen," he said. "When I turned on the lights of my car, I saw that the whole of San Pedro had fallen down."

In El Progresso, eighteen-year-old Alfonso Amaya Montes heard his sister call, then found himself buried under a pile of tiles and adobe, all that remained of his parents' house.

"I thought of my father and mother and wondered whether they would be saved," he said. Choking with dust, he had just enough breath to call out. An hour later, a man with white hair managed to dig him out. Then he discovered that his parents and the sister that had called out to him were all dead.

"I lost eleven relatives," he said. "They

"At such a moment, you feel very lonely."

were buried without coffins, wrapped only in sheets. We could not have funerals. There were too many dead."

They could not even call for help. The phone lines were down and the roads out of town were blocked by landslides. At dawn a messenger set off on foot for Zacapa, thirty-seven miles away.

In the capital, Guatemala City, Father Constantino Gastino heard "a sound like an explosion – perhaps an entrance of thieves" to his seventeenth century church of Cerrito del Carmen. Another man compared it to the sound of an express train. Luis Arturo Elaena was woken by the sound of screams and crashing furniture. Then the roof fell in on him and he was unconscious again.

In the west of the city, a bakery collapsed, demolishing the adjoining houses and killing seven people. Student Estuardo Nanne climbed out his bedroom window and clung onto the window sill while his neighbour's house came crashing down.

"At such a moment, you feel very lonely," he said.

In Guatemala City, the electricity is automatically cut off during severe earthquakes to prevent fire, plunging the capital into darkness. But this was no handicap to lottery-ticket seller René Quiñones and his wife, who are both blind.

"We had been taught how to take care of ourselves," he said. He had his wife keep their clothes on a chair beside the bed and had taught their children to do the same. "Darkness was no obstacle."

Don Claudio Urrutia, a seismologist from Guatemala National Observatory, was woken by his wife.

"She is my first seismograph," he said. "We had just felt the P [primary], but not the S [secondary shock wave]. I bent over to get my shoes and toppled onto the floor with the shock of the S. Everything was dark and moving, so I felt the wall and reached the door. I found my wife there. She had also fallen, so I picked her up and got her outside and said: 'Don't move.' Then I went back

inside to get a flashlight. And then my pistol. And then my wallet – if your house falls down, you need money. After that I went to the observatory. You know, other people run outside when an earthquake starts. Scientists run inside, to make sure their instruments are working."

Father Constantino was equally professional.

"I pulled on my pants, then asked God for his help," he said.

Fearful of aftershocks, doctors and nurses moved their patients out onto the sidewalks.

"I've never seen so many fractured spines and pelvises," said one surgeon. "Everyone was in bed then their houses fell on them."

Another doctor reported suturing thirty-six spleens in twenty-four hours.

There were no beds for the children. They had to lie on the street while doctors and nurses attended to them on their knees. That night was cold and they only had one blanket apiece. The next day, the medical staff found they had a new problem. Indian children were brought in from the highlands. They only spoke Cakchiquel, so the nurses could not find out their names or the name of their home villages.

"Travelling through the city," wrote one reporter, "the damage you see gets worse the poorer the district is. When you come to the slums that straggle down the ravines at the edge of town – the barrios – hundreds of little landslides had taken twenty or thirty houses at a time, tumbling to the bottom of the ravine, collapsed like a pack of cards. I spoke to one old man who had lived through this nightmare. His house had been the one at the top."

Looting began. Gunfire was heard, then the radio station issued a warning about "false medical helpers". They were giving injured victims a shot of morphine, then robbing them while they were unconscious.

In all 58,000 houses had been destroyed in Guatemala City. The fault

> "I pulled on my pants, then asked God for his help."

line could be traced for 150 miles with individual cracks thirty-three feet long and four inches wide.

One Indian remarked stoically: "You go to sleep and wake, and the world has changed."

Chile 1960

Occupying a long sliver of land between the Pacific Ocean and the Andes, Chile has experienced numerous earthquakes. One of the worst happened on 24 January 1939, when an area of 400 square miles was hit, killing around 50,000 people, mostly children.

The provincial capital of Concepción, some 260 miles south of Santiago, was flattened. In Chillán, a city of 50,000 people fifty miles inland which had previously been levelled by an earthquake in 1853, only three buildings out of 140 city blocks were left standing. Over 10,000 were dead. The Municipal movie theatre, packed with a thousand people, collapsed without warning, killing everyone inside. The *New York Times* reported: "Indescribable terror was pictured on the faces of the dead when some of the bodies were removed."

The governor's palace collapsed on passing cars. Outlying towns were destroyed. A coal mine collapsed on the miners underground and more than a dozen cathedrals were destroyed. Six provinces, home to 1.6 million – a third of Chile's population – were affected. The needles on seismographs shot off the scale and tremors could be felt in neighbouring Argentina and 1,500 miles away on the Peruvian border.

The piers at the local ports were destroyed and relief planes had to air drop supplies. Pilots reported that what they could see of Chillán was nothing more than "a vast antheap, with jagged lengths of church towers and other masonry protruding". They saw "corpses lined up in the blistering sun, evidently

awaiting identification by relatives who may never be found". But the heat of the Chilean summer was itself a danger and witnesses spoke of the "bodies of victims being tossed into pits in a feverish effort to dispose of them before disease sets in". Drinking water soon became "so scarce that schoolchildren, parched by the intense heat, were receiving it only by the spoonful".

It was only three days after the earthquake that the British cruisers *Ajax* and *Exeter* turned up. Marines went ashore as relief parties, while the *Exeter* ferried more than six hundred survivors north to Valparaíso.

The volcano overlooking Chillán began to glow red, as if about to erupt and a local municipal official suggested that, like Pompeii, the ruins should be abandoned and the city rebuilt elsewhere. The volcano did not erupt, though several others in the region did.

The following day, a violent storm broke. According to the *New York Times*, 100,000 rain-soaked refugees were soon "trying to push northwards ahead of the icy winds from the Andes. Shelter was impossible… thousands of the injured, insufficiently wrapped in blankets, lay under the trees".

After four days, a boy of twelve who had been trapped with his dog was dug out. But most of the trapped had to be abandoned due to lack of manpower. "Thousands of other voices crazily demanding aid have gradually died away and today are silent," reported the *Times*. "The survivors have abandoned all hope of seeing their missing relatives again. They no longer shed tears. They do not even talk."

With thousands of rotting corpses beyond the reach of rescue teams, the destruction of Chillán was completed with dynamite and quick lime.

Along with the 50,000 dead, there were 60,000 injured and 700,000 homeless. Thousands of orphans roamed the area and Chile's richest farmland had been laid waste.

This same area was struck again on 22

> "Indescribable terror was pictured on the faces of the dead…"

The quake caused mines to collapse, trapping workers underground

May 1960, when the largest earthquake on record occurred off the Arauco Peninsula, forty miles south of Concepción. It had a magnitude of 8.6 on the Richter scale, but the focus was at a depth of twenty miles. Even so 2,290 people were killed and $500 million worth of damage was done. Concepción was shattered and in the city of Valdivia to the south one in every three houses were destroyed.

Landslides caused lakes to overflow, inundating surrounding farm land. In other places subsidence caused an inrush of water, while other areas were elevated by up to seven feet. Inland the intensity of the earthquake caused soil to liquefy and houses simply fell down. In one place the liquefied soil flowed into a harbour, trapping ships at anchor.

The dormant volcano Puyehue nearby sprang back into life two days later, shooting a cloud of ash and steam 20,000 feet into the air, and hot springs in the area were turned into "mud volcanoes".

The earthquake caused a tsunami over eighty feet high, hurling debris up to two miles in land up the Chilean coast. But the Chileans were prepared and had evacuated the coastal strip. Some, however, returned home before a fourth wave hit and were killed.

The tsunami set out across the Pacific Ocean at a speed of 400 miles an hour. When it struck Hilo in Hawaii fourteen hours after the initial shock, the waves were still thirty-four feet high. Sixty-one people were killed, 282 injured and $24 million worth of damage done.

Eight hours later, when the tsunami reached Japan it was just twelve feet high. But this was enough to hurl large fishing boats 150 feet inland. One hundred and eighty people were killed. There was $450 million worth of property damage done and the livelihoods of 150,000 people were affected. Another 258 people were killed in the Philippines.

Back in Chile the earthquake and tsunami had left 100,000 people homeless. There were food riots which were dispersed by the army and a six-year-old boy had his heart torn from his body by Mapuche Indians to placate the god of the sea.

Peru 1970

At 3.23 pm on 31 May 1970, a fault ruptured under the Pacific floor some fifteen miles off the coast of Peru. The shock registered 7.75 on the Richter scale. The resulting earthquake set off avalanches and landslides in the Andes, which killed some 66,794 people and left more than half a million people homeless.

The worst by far occurred on the slopes of Nevado de Huascarán, Peru's highest mountain, some seventy miles inland. The shaking lasted forty-five seconds. Then there was a loud explosion as a giant part of western slope broke away. A slab of ice and rock as much as 100 feet thick, covering the side of the mountain from 18,000 to 21,000 feet, fell over 1,000 feet before it hit the lower slopes scoping up more rock and snow. This created an avalanche over seven miles long. Some 2.5 billion cubic feet of snow, ice, rock and mud travelling at up to 210 miles an hour slid into the Rio Santa Valley, burying over 25,000 people. The town of Ranrahirca was completely obliterated. A mile away the resort of Yungay was buried beneath a hundred foot of debris. Boulders weighing several tons each crashed on down the valley. Houses would explode when the rocks hit them and they left bomb craters in their wake. This was the most destructive landslide on record.

Peru suffers regularly from catastrophic earthquakes due to the collision of the South American crustal plate with the Nazca crustal plate, which is located under the Pacific Ocean to the west of South America. An earthquake on 13-15 August 1863 is believed to have killed 25,000. Another 25,000 were thought to

Houses would explode when the rocks hit them...

have died in the region in 1892. Some 200 to 300 were killed by an earthquake in Lima on 25 May 1940, with another 5,000 reporting injuries in the port of Callao. An earthquake in the department of Ancash to the north claimed some 700 lives in 10-13 November 1946 and over 100 were killed in the Cuzco earthquake of 12 May 1950. On 13 January 1960, strong earthquakes killed more than 2,000 people and did hundreds of millions of pounds worth of damage.

Then on 25 April 1974, a giant landslide caused an earthquake, rather than the other way around. The collapse of a mountainside around the Mantaro River sent out a tremor which measured 4.5 on the Richter scale.

San Francisco 1906

The quake of 1906 earned San Francisco the name of "Earthquake City". This was not because of the great loss of life. There were an estimated 2,000 casualties, small beer compared to the death toll in other major quakes. But the United States had not experienced an earthquake on this scale before.

At the time, San Francisco was barely sixty years old and it had already become a world-famous metropolis. Known as "the American Paris", it was the most important city west of the Mississippi. A financial, commercial and cultural centre, it was the western terminal of the transcontinental railroad. It was America's gateway to the Orient and, in terms of foreign and domestic trade, it was second only to New York.

San Francisco not only sits beside the San Andreas fault, which runs up the coast of California. There is another fault, the Hayward fault, that runs up the east side of the bay. The original mission at Yerba Buena was hit by earthquakes in

"Then came a sickening swaying of the earth that threw us flat on our faces."

June and July 1808, 1822, 1836 and 1838. Four years after Yerba Buena was renamed San Francisco in 1847, several buildings were damaged. Another earthquake hit the following year which cracked the ground so severely that Lake Merced drained into the sea.

In 1856, an earthquake disturbed the waters of the bay and was felt sixty miles inland at Stockton. An earthquake broke store windows in San Francisco on 1864. The following year a number of buildings were destroyed and a crack two blocks long opened up on Howard Street. In 1868, an earthquake centred near San Leandro on the other side of the bay damaged every building in nearby Hayward and was felt over 150 miles away. Mark Twain was in San Francisco at the time and noted how many people suffered from motion sickness. Some were incapacitated for days. Even so, nothing prepared the residents of the city by the bay for what happened in 1906.

At 5.13am on 18 April 1906, a massive earthquake, estimated at 8.2 on the Richter scale, struck San Francisco. The first tremor lasted about forty seconds. A second lasted a minute and a half.

Police sergeant Jesse Cook saw it coming. Hearing a deep rumble, he looked up.

"The whole of the street was undulating," he said. "It was as if the waves of the ocean were coming towards me."

Another witness said it reminded him of a rat being shaken by a terrier.

John Barrett, news editor of the *San Francisco Examiner*, had just finished his shift and was standing on Market Street with two reporters.

"Suddenly we found ourselves staggering and reeling," he said. "It was as if the earth were slipping gently from under our feet. Then came a sickening swaying of the earth that threw us flat on our faces."

Although they struggled they could not get to their feet.

"I looked in a dazed fashion around me," he continued. "I saw for an instant

RUINS OF

The quake of 1906 earned San Francisco the nickname 'Earthquake City'

E CITY AFTER EARTHQUAKE AND FIRE 1906.
SAN FRANCISCO. CAL.

In the wake of the tremors many buildings would have to be pulled down to be made safe

the big buildings in what looked like a crazy dance. Then it seemed as though my head were split with the roar that crashed into my ears. Big buildings were crumbling as one might crush a biscuit in one's hand... Storms of masonry rained into the street. Wild, high jangles of smashing glass cut a sharp note into the frightful roaring. Ahead of me a great cornice crushed a man as if he were a maggot – a labourer in overalls on his way to the Union Iron Works, with a dinner pail under his arm... It seemed a quarter of an hour until it stopped. As a matter of fact, it lasted three minutes. Footing grew firm again, but hardly were we on our feet before we were sent reeling again by repeated shocks, but they were milder.

Clinging to something, one could stand."

Church bells clanged. Wood-framed house splintered. Pipes twisted. Fissures opened in the streets. Electrical wires gave off showers of blue sparks. Water mains burst and gas rose out of cracks in the street.

"From the south of us, faint, but all too clear, came a horrible chorus of human cries of agony," said Barrett. "Down there in the ramshackle section of the city, the wretched houses had fallen upon the sleeping families. Down there, throughout the day the fire burned... That was what came next – the fire. It shot up everywhere. The fierce wave of destruction had carried a flaming torch with it – agony, death and a flaming torch. It was just as if some fire demon was rushing from place to place with such a torch."

The Italian tenor Enrico Caruso was in town to sing in San Francisco's Grand Opera House. He was staying at the eight-hundred-room Palace Hotel on Market Street.

"I woke up, feeling my bed rocking as though I am in a ship," he said. "From the window I see buildings shaking, big pieces of masonry falling. I run into the street. That night I sleep on the hard ground – my legs ache yet from so rough a bed."

Also in town, at the St Francis Hotel, was the matinee idol John Barrymore who was listed "missing" for two days. In fact, he had emerged from the ruins of his hotel, complaining of a hangover, and set out on one of his legendary drinking binges.

Across the street from the Palace, the chief of the Postal Telegraph Cable Company sent out the first news of the earthquake at 6 am. The wire he sent read:

THERE WAS AN EARTHQUAKE AT FIVE FIFTEEN THIS MORNING, WRECKING SEVERAL BUILDINGS AND WRECKING OUR OFFICES. THEY ARE CARTING DEAD FROM THE FALLEN BUILDINGS. FIRE ALL OVER TOWN. THERE IS NO WATER AND WE HAVE LOST OUR POWER. I'M GOING TO GET OUT OF THE OFFICE AS WE HAVE HAD A LITTLE SHAKE EVERY FEW MINUTES."

Collapsing brick chimneys destroyed San Francisco's numerous wood-framed houses. In one small hotel eight guests were killed – not all of them from the earthquake itself. Many were said to have drowned when the ground floor was flooded by a burst water main.

Within half-an-hour of the quake, more than fifty fires had started. Stoves fell over, spilling their hot coals. A cooking fire on Market Street burnt out of control. Electrical sparks set wood on fire and escaping gas ignited. Soon these separate fires merged into one inferno as ninety per cent of the buildings were made of wood or wood sheathed in brick. By early evening the fires had reached Chinatown – the biggest in the US – and were threatening the rich people's mansions on Nob Hill.

The flames were so intense that steel beams melted and silver coins in banks fused into ingots. Afterwards safes had to be left for days to cool down before they were opened. Otherwise, the air would rush in, turning paper money and important documents to ashes.

San Francisco was famed for its fire service. It had eight stations and 585 firemen. Unfortunately, it was without a fire chief. Awoken by the quake, he had stepped out of his bedroom door in the dark. But the landing had collapsed and he had fallen three storeys, fracturing his arms, legs, ribs and skulls. He died five days later without regaining consciousness.

The army took over. Under the orders of President Theodore Roosevelt, General Funston mobilised two thousand troops from the Presidio. They were deployed two to a block the length of Market Street to prevent looting. But there was little trouble that first night.

"Remarkable as it may seem," wrote author Jack London in *Collier's Weekly*, "Wednesday night, while the whole city

"the wretched houses had fallen upon the sleeping families."

crashed and roared into ruin, was a quiet night. There was no shouting and yelling. There was no hysteria, no disorder… Before the flames, throughout the night, fled tens of thousands of homeless ones. Some were wrapped in blankets. Others carrying bundles of bedding and dear household treasures. Sometimes a whole family was harnessed to a carriage or delivery wagon that was weighted down with their possessions."

Retiring to safety out in the bay, London watched as the flames spread.

"East, west, north, and south," he wrote, "strong winds were blowing upon the doomed city."

By dawn the following day, flames were engulfing the Barbary Coast, San Francisco's famous red light district that boasted a thousand saloons and posh restaurants offering "supper bedrooms" on the upper floors. The army tried to halt the flames using explosives to create firebreaks, but the gun powder started more fires. They even resorted to shelling, but nothing worked.

Those fleeing the city were strangely subdued as if stunned or drugged. Another eyewitness, psychologist William James, was impressed by people's composure and their kindness.

"Not a single whine or plaintive word did I hear from the hundred losers whom I spoke to," he said. "Instead of that there was a temper of helpfulness beyond the counting."

The Southern Pacific charged no fare to carry the refugees away. Some 300,000 homeless people camped out in the parks. The army created tent cities overnight. Prisoners were sent to work digging latrines and graves. Food was brought in on relief trains that had priority over all other traffic, while lost children were taken to a transit camp in Oakland.

By the afternoon of 19 April, the whole city east of Van Ness Avenue was on fire. Van Ness ran north-south and separated the old city from the newer developments, including the Western Addition which housed 150,000 rich people. The avenue was 125 feet wide,

the widest in the city. General Funston decided that this was where he would have to stop the fire, otherwise the whole city would be lost. The buildings along the east side of Van Ness were evacuated. With artillery, kerosene and dynamite, he demolished them, making a firebreak 175 feet wide and one mile – sixteen city blocks – long.

On the afternoon of the 20th, the flames reached the firebreak. The heat was so intense that the paint on the house on the west side of Van Ness began to bubble and crack. Then suddenly the wind changed. The western part of the city had been saved. Now the wharves – San Francisco's economic lifeline – were under threat. But navy fireboats and the city's fire engines pumped salt water from the bay and managed to dowse the flames.

The last fire was extinguished at 7.45 am on the 21st. The centre of the city had been gutted. In all 28,188 buildings covering 512 blocks – or 2,800 acres – had been destroyed. The entire business and commercial district had been burnt out. Every downtown store had been destroyed and only one bank remained standing. Market Street was just a footpath through the debris. The steel frame of City Hall remained standing, though its stone cladding had fallen off. The US Mint building had also been saved due to the fact that it had been ringed by troops during the fire after rumours spread that thieves planned to steal the $200 million that was on the premises.

Nearly three-quarters of the city had to be rebuilt or extensively repaired. Insurance claims totalled $229 million – that's the equivalent of $4.2 billion at the year 2000 prices. No one knows how much uninsured property was lost.

As San Franciscans returned to their homes, there were problems meeting their most basic needs. Water could not be pumped into the reservoirs because over 23,000 household taps had been left open and sewage leaked into the cracked water mains. Fires could not be lit in

"East, west, north, and south, strong winds were blowing upon the doomed city."

All that remained of most of San Francisco's buildings was a barely recognisable shell

houses until their chimney had be certified as safe, so all cooking had to be done out of doors – and there was a shortage of utensils. Gas and electricity could not be turned back on until all the houses in the district had been inspected.

Over $9 million in aid flowed in from around the country. The Japanese Red Cross sent $245,000 and the Empress of China $45,000. Crews got to work twenty-four hours a day, seven days a week, clearing the rubble. Most of it was

"Not a single whine or plaintive word did I hear..."

Roads became impassable as whole streets collapsed

dumped into the shallows of the bay. It was later built on, extending the city out beyond the original shoreline.

Businesses reopened within a week, with shops and offices taking over the large houses that had been saved along the west side of Van Ness. In two months, over 8,000 large wooden huts – each housing six to eight families – were erected. The troops returned to their barracks on 1 July. On 5 July, the saloons started serving again and the breadlines ended on 1 August.

By the following spring the rubble had gone. The city was rebuilt on the same layout as before, though the city planners now included a system of reservoirs, secondary water mains and cisterns to fight any future fire. By 1909, 20,000 new houses had been built, with construction workers being paid three times the going rate. And in 1915 San Francisco hosted the Panama-Pacific Exposition, celebrating the opening of the Panama Canal – as it had announced it would in 1905.

San Francisco was hit again in 1989 by an earthquake that did $10 billion-worth of damage – the single most expensive natural disaster in US history. At 5.04 pm on 17 October, a tremor measuring 7.1 on the Richter scale struck. It epicentre was near the Loma Prieta mountain fifty miles to the south. The Marina district in the northern part of the city was heavily damaged. It was built on landfill laid down in the early part of the century, which liquefied during the quake, and a ruptured gas main started a fire, which was brought under control in a matter of hours. The Mission, Haight, Sunset and Tenderloin districts were all damaged. A fifty-foot section of the upper deck of the Bay Bridge fell on the lower deck. Dozens of drivers were killed when the 1.5-mile upper section of Interstate 880 in Oakland know and the Cypress Viaduct collapsed on the lower one. Other highways around the city were closed by cracks and landslides. In all sixty-seven people died.

Kashmir 2005

Awesome and treacherous, the disputed region of Kashmir squats at the western edge of the Himalayas in southern Asia between India and Pakistan. Until 8 October 2005 the greatest threat to its populace had been terrorists operating in the region and the squabbling Indian and Pakistani governments squaring up to one another, apparently poised to brandish nuclear weapons.

However, destruction of far greater proportions was let loose when an earthquake struck early that morning, sparking a continental catastrophe. The 'quake was not excessively large – measuring about 7.6 on the Richter scale – but it occurred closer to the earth's crust than usual. Fervour over the political situation was for a while reduced to ashes, along with the homes and hopes of millions.

The tremors began as Kashmiri students sat at their desks, ready for another day of study. Entire classes were wiped out in the few seconds it took for the planet to rupture as India was pushed by nature's relentless subterranean forces into Asia. People also died in their homes as the earthquake brought high rise buildings to rubble in the regional capital of Muzaffarabad and flattened long-established settlements in distant and remote areas. It took weeks to assess the death toll but official figures released within a month of the disaster put it at about 75,000, the vast majority in the area controlled by Pakistan. Tens of thousands were injured and a staggering 3.3 million people were homeless.

Terrifying aftershocks left survivors too panicked to take shelter in their suddenly unstable world. Alas, their trauma was only just beginning as the infrastructure of their communities had entirely collapsed. The quake fractured roads that could have led people to hospitals, food and emergency shelters, and even tracks and footpaths were at risk of

If the injured were not down from the villages before the winter snows began, the number of dead was set to swell inexorably.

subsidence or landslides. Injured people were compelled to wait in agony for evacuation by helicopter, with food, warmth and water becoming scarce. The alternative was a hazardous trek to safety as the Pakistani army had just 19 helicopters at its disposal to move thousands of people. Communications were difficult or impossible. Burial of the dead appeared an insurmountable task.

Soon domestic and international aid began to roll in. However, large lorries leased to carry supplies soon clogged those highways that were still accessible, blocking routes for ambulances and refugees heading out. Helicopters including giant Chinooks made forays into remote regions to make drops of food, water and tents. All too often, the crews watched helplessly as the vital supplies bounced down the mountainside into ravines, out of reach of the desperate. It was mules that ultimately provided the most reliable mode of transport around the shattered region. By whatever means, relief for the isolated villages was painfully slow in arriving.

Seasonal rains hindered the rescue efforts. But it was the threat of winter that was causing serious concern to both relief workers and the surviving population. If the injured were not down from the villages before the snows and sufficient quantities of food not delivered to remote areas the number of dead was set to swell inexorably. A shortage of tents and medical supplies some four weeks after the earthquake finally persuaded the Pakistani president Pervez Musharraf to call on the international community for a re-doubling of its efforts to assist Kashmir's suffering and vulnerable population.

Initially, old enemies India and Pakistan seemed ready to co-operate to help victims. Kashmiris themselves have long resented the territorial lines that parted them from family and friends and were delighted with the prospect of crossing the fiercely guarded borders. Ultimately, diplomacy broke down and thousands have been left not knowing if relatives on the other side of the front line are alive or dead. As 2005 came to a close, the UN estimated that around 3 million Kashmiris were still homeless as a result of the quake, with anything up to 800,000 sleeping out in the open. As winter closed in, their hopes lay in effective co-operation between national and regional authorities and organizations operating in the region for the delivery of emergency supplies of food and water and tents suitable for the harsh Himalayan conditions. Without this co-operation, and a massive influx of the foreign aid promised but yet to fully materialize, the people stranded on the mountainsides of Kashmir were doomed.

Suffer the children: innocent victim of the Kashmir tragedy

Amidst the ruins of what was once her home, a Kashmiri woman contemplates a bleak future.

Tsunami

Papua New Guinea 1998

On 17 July 1998 three mountainous waves pounded the northern coastline of Papua New Guinea, carrying away at least 2,500 people. Debris hanging from the tops of palm trees indicated that the waves reached heights of forty-six feet, taller than a four-storey building. According to Costas Synolakis, head of a team of researchers at the University of South California, it was "about double the worst overland flow that we had seen before".

The tremor that caused the tsunami measured 7.1 on the Richter scale – a strong but not usual quake. Tremors of at least this size strike somewhere on the globe about every three weeks. No houses were destroyed by the earthquake itself and people who lived only ten miles from the most devastated area said that the shaking was not particularly intense. The earthquake occurred approximately 45 miles (70 km) Southeast of Vanimo, New Guinea, PNG, at 08:49 GMT on July 17, 1998 (6:49 PM local time in Papua New Guinea).

According to the National Earthquake Information Service (NEIS) of the U. S. Geological Survey, the epicentre was 3.08 S, 141.76 E (about 12 miles off the shore of Papua). A major aftershock followed, less than an hour later. Synolakis says that the earthquake itself could not have generated such a large wave and believes that it triggered an underwater landslide that in turn generated the giant waves. A nearby cliff showed signs of a fresh avalanche and it is thought that a much larger slide happened underwater where the seafloor plunges steeply into the submarine trench that runs off the north coast of New Guinea.

Survivors of the disaster describe seeing a wall of water barrelling toward shore. But unlike a normal wave with a crest, this tsunami was like a plateau of water, averaging thirty feet high and extending three miles from front to back. The leading wave arrived five to ten minutes after the earthquake. It swept over the shore at speeds of up to twelve miles an hour for more than a minute, before draining away ready for the next wave, which followed several minutes later.

The New Guinea tsunami was particularly devastating because it struck just twelve miles of coastline, unlike other tsunamis that are spread over hundreds. It also hit a particularly vulnerable section of the north coast, where a thousand-foot wide strip of land separates the ocean from a brackish lagoon, which itself was left by a tsunami in 1907. The families of fishermen living on this sand bar had no way to escape the waves. The water washed away all trace of the houses there.

Synolakis warns that similar underwater landslides could occur anywhere along the west coast of the United States from California to southern Alaska.

Like other countries vulnerable to tsunamis, Papua New Guinea is home to considerable seismic activity. In 1951, Mount Lamington erupted, unleashing a cloud of superheated dust and steam which laid waste some ninety square miles of land and incinerating nearly three thousand people. The explosion was heard two hundred miles to the north on New Britain. Survivors suffered severe burns and all vegetation was turned charcoal. Earthquakes and mudflows contributed another 3,000 casualties. Valleys around the volcano were

the waves reached heights of forty-six feet

The sandbar separating the Bismarck Sea from the Sissano lagoon. Tthere is now no trace of the village which once stood on the sandbar.

filled with ash that remained hot for months and wood trapped underneath it would catch fire when exposed to air for months afterwards. The eruption continued for several months, building a dome of over 1,800 feet at a rate of up to four feet an hour.

Mount Rabaul began erupting in 1797. Further eruptions occurred in 1791 and 1850. During that time, the uplift caused by the magma chamber of the volcano lifted a nearby coral reef out of the water. An eruption on 4 February 1878 caused tsunamis of its own when the ground along the coast near Tavurvur was raise by as much as twenty feet in places, while subsidence at Davapia Rocks put some homes underwater. Between 1916 and 1919 a number of volcanoes in the area erupted. Then on

28 May 1937, the area was shaken by earthquakes. Buildings collapsed and landslides generated tsunamis. A reef was lifted clear of the water, submerged and exposed again, all within ten minutes. A deadly pyroclastic flow killed five hundred people and carbon dioxide given off killed birds and animals for months to come. Toxic sulphur dioxide and hydrogen chloride were given off in 1938. There were explosive eruptions of steam in 1941, followed by a major earthquake and more emissions of sulphur dioxide and hydrogen chloride. Earthquakes continued for the next three years. Another major quake shocked the area in 1967. And between 1971 and 1983 they occurred at a rate of two a day.

Off the coast of Papua New Guinea lies

the volcanic island of Karkar, which has erupted ten times since the mid-seventeenth century. In 1643, a huge flame was seen to appear from its summit. It was shaken by earthquakes in 1895 and 1930, then an explosive eruption occurred in 1962. Lava flows began in 1974. By 1978 ground temperatures were so high that the island was incandescent. The following year an explosive eruption of steam killed two vulcanologists.

Philippines 1976

A little after midnight on 23 August 1976, an earthquake measuring eight on the Richter scale struck the southern Philippines. It lasted just twenty seconds. On the island of Mindanao, the coastal settlements of Alicia, Cotabato, Davao and Pagadian City were hit, causing extensive damaged. But that was not the worst of the inhabitants' troubles.

The epicentre of the quake was beneath the Sulawesi Sea. The dazed residents of the coastal cities were just digging themselves out when a tsunami hit. The wave was thirty feet high. Nearly 8,000 people died, mostly from drowning. Another 2,000 were injured and 90,000 were left homeless.

In 1960, the Chilean earthquake generated a massive tsunami which pounded the Philippines with waves of 15 to 35 feet high. And in 1572, the eruption of the Philippine volcano Taal on the central island of Luzon caused a tsunami in the lake from which the cone rises. Taal has erupted thirty times since 1572. Luzon has numerous active volcanoes including Mayon which has erupted forty times since 1616, generating both lava flows and clouds of superheated steam and dust.

There are other active volcanoes in the Philippines – Apo and Cottobato on Mindanao, Malaspina on the island of

Negros and Camaguin ninety miles to the south-west, which erupted in 1876.

The archipelago is also shaken by earthquakes. On 3 July 1863, Manila was badly damaged. Hospitals, churches and government buildings fell down. The death toll was around a thousand. The damage to the tobacco industry alone ran to $2 million. Another earthquake hit Manila in 1880. Though there was widespread destruction throughout the city, no loss of life was reported. Then in 1991, Mount Pinatubo erupted (*see* page 161).

Japan 1933

On 3 March 1933, an earthquake variously measured as 8.6 or 8.9 on the Richter scale occurred a hundred miles off the east coast of Japan, on the landward side of the Japan Trench at about 2,000 fathoms. The shock itself had little effect on the Japanese island of Honshu, except to alert the authorities to the dangers. But they delayed.

A warning was broadcast at the last moment. But some warning was better than none. The coastal dwellers evacuated the area, but they had to get well inland to be safe. The tsunami that hit the coast of Sanriku province – ripping up all 220 miles of it – was seventy-five feet high. Some 3,000 people died, 9,000 homes destroyed and 8,000 boats smashed to pieces.

Survivors of the disaster also noted a curious phenomenon. The tsunami hit at night, but the oncoming wave was lit up with flashes of bright light. This was caused by hundreds of thousands of tiny creatures called *Noctilus miliaris*, whose flagella are bioluminescent due to the presence of organic phosphorous.

The island of Honshu is particularly vulnerable to tsunami as it is one extruded node of the fractured spine of Japan and is riven by deep faults both longitudinally and latitudinally from end

Survivors noted a curious phenomenon.

to end, as is the seabed surrounding the island. One of the most active faults splits the floor of the Gulf of Sagami to the south-east.

Japan 1896

In 1896, Charles F. Richter had not introduced his scale and there was no system to broadcast earthquake warnings. But for those who could read the signs on the east coast of Japan, there were clear indications that a tsunami was on its way.

On 15 June, the coastal towns of Sanriku province were packed as people were celebrating a Shinto holiday with parades and pageants. Heavy rain had been falling all day, but by early evening the skies started to clear. Then came the first hint of danger. At around 7.30 pm there were a series of long-lasting tremors that seemed to rumble underfoot. Seismic activity is commonplace in Japan and nobody took any notice. But for those who knew of such things, the long duration of the tremors told of a great submarine earthquake some ninety-three miles out to sea.

About twenty minutes later, the first sure sign that a tsunami was on its way came. The sea suddenly pulled back from the shore, leaving fish stranded, flapping on the mud. Boats were torn from the moorings and washed out to sea by the speed of the retreating tide. This is commonly seen before a tsunami strikes.

Out to sea there was a booming noise. It grew louder like the creeping barrage of a thousand cannons. It was only then that the revellers began to take notice. But it was too late. A mountain of water at least one hundred feet high came rushing towards them at a speed of up to 500 miles an hour.

A few were saved by the merest chance. A number of old men had gone up to the top of a cliff to play Go, away from the bustle of the festival. A handful of babies were saved. Their parents had

"the unconquerable stench of death"

fled from the waves, dumped their tots on high ground and gone back to pick up older offspring. But almost everyone perished.

According to records of the time: "Of the entire population of the towns and villages that up to the moment of disaster were thriving with life, not one of the population or a vestige remained. On the other hand, the fishermen who at the time were some distance out at sea and had noticed nothing unusual were, on their way home the next morning, amazed to find the sea for miles strewn with house wreckage and floating corpses. They then realised for the first time the tragedy that had been enacted the night before."

Those at sea rarely notice a tsunami passing under them. The deadly wave may only be two feet high from crest to trough, but it is of such a length – usually many tens of miles long – that it carried a great deal of water. This only builds into a mountain when it is slowed by shallow water. The Japanese word "tsu" means harbour and "ami" means wave.

A correspondent for *Harper's Weekly* visited soon after and found the coast devoid of life for thirty miles and estimated that 30,000 people had been killed. A samurai, hearing what he took to be cannon, rushed to get his sword to fight off imagined invaders. When his body was found, he was still clutching the sword.

A French missionary was lost in the inundation. Two of his colleagues set out to find his body to give him a Christian burial. They were forced to give up. The reporter for *Harper's* noted: "It was necessary to build fires to destroy the evidence of putrefaction because there were no disinfectants procurable." Hanging over the land for days, he said, were "the unconquerable stench of death and the smoke of the funeral fires".

Official government casualties were given as "10,617 houses swept away, 2,456 houses partly demolished, 27,122 persons killed and 9,247 persons injured".

The wave was 100 feet high and travelling at a speed of 500 miles an hour.

Japan & Sumatra 1883

The eruption of Krakatoa on 27 August 1883 was not unexpected. The three-cone volcano in the Sunda Strait between the Indonesian islands of Java and Sumatra had been active for some time. Indeed, the whole region was active. More than seventy-six peaks in the Indonesian archipelago had been active since records had been kept. And in 1815, Tambora in eastern Indonesia had erupted, killing 90,000 people in the resulting tsunami and famine.

Krakatoa was the remnant of a prehistoric volcano, whose eruption had shaped the Sunda Strait. The original 6,000-foot high cone had been blasted into dust. New outpourings of lava and ash piled up a new cone half-a-mile high, which combined with two smaller cones to make Krakatoa Island.

In 1680, the smallest cone, Perboewatan, had erupted, stripping the island of its vegetation. The jungle grew back and for two hundred years it seemed to be extinct. Then in early May 1883, tremors were felt. On 20 May, Perboewatan started thundering. "Booming sounds, like the firing of artillery" were heard in Batavia – now Jakarta – ninety-eight miles to the east. The German warship *Elisabeth* saw a plume of vapour that resembled "a giant head of cauliflower" and was covered in ash. The mail packet *Governor General Loudon* took a party of tourists from Batavia to see the column of vapour that now rose to 10,000 feet with a firey glow at its base. Some went ashore on the beach that was now covered in ash and pumice. A few reckless souls even climbed the cinder cone to peer into the crater itself.

Activity then ceased, only to resume on 16 June. By the end of July the authorities were becoming concerned. Captain H.J.G. Ferzenaar of the Dutch colonial survey department went to Krakatoa to

> "Booming sounds, like the firing of artillery"

assess the situation. He found that the second largest cone, Danan, had now opened. The island had been stripped of vegetation again and he advised against further visits.

Then at 1 pm on Sunday 26 August 1883 a series of massive explosions shook the island every ten minutes or so. By 2 pm the vapour plume had reached seventeen miles. By dusk the cloud had spread over an area of 125 square miles. Arcs of static electricity wreathed the cone which emitted lethal, superheated gas, ash, cinder, stone and mud.

On board the sailing ship *Charles Bal*, bound from Belfast to Hong Kong via the Strait of Sunda, Captain W.J.Watson recorded in his log: "Chains of fire appeared to ascend and descend between the island and the sky. The blinding fall of sand and stones, the intense blackness above and around us, broken only by the incessant glare of varied kinds of lightning, and the continued explosive roars of Krakatoa, made our situation a truly awful one."

The *Charles Bal* made it through the Strait. It is estimated that 6,500 craft didn't, victims of the debris falling from the sky and the tsunamis the eruption generated. That evening three feet of water in Telok Betong, the port in Sumatra's Lampong Bay, swept on the pier, beaching all the vessels in the harbour. Six foot of water hit Merak on Java, flooding a Chinese encampment and drowning its inhabitants.

After each surge the water would recede, then return with even more force. Waves between fifty and 130 feet were recorded. The lighthouses along the Sunda Strait were toppled. The Sumatran town of Kalimbang was swamped to a depth of eighty feet. Sebesi Island to the north of Krakatoa was completely submerged, drowning all its 3,000 inhabitants. By the time Merak was hit for the third time, the hundred or so survivors remaining were huddled in the stone houses at the top of a 135-foot cliff. The giant waves simply demolished

Krakatoa is one of history's most famous volcanoes

them. Only two of the town's 3,000 residents survived.

The *Governor General Loudon* was moored off Telok Betong when the tsunami hit.

"At about 7 am a tremendous wave came moving in from the sea, which blocked the view and moved with tremendous speed," said a passenger. The ship was "lifted up with a dizzying rapidity. The ship made a formidable leap, and immediately afterwards we felt as though we had plunged into the abyss." As for the port: "All was finished. There, where a few moments ago lived Telok Betong, was nothing but open sea."

At 10.02 am Krakatoa exploded with the loudest noise ever heard by human ear. The explosion was mistaken for rifle shots some 2,250 miles away in central Australia. The police chief on the island of Rodriguez 3,000 miles away in the Indian Ocean said that the sound resembled "the distant roar of heavy guns". The sound had taken four hours to get there.

Exploding with the force of one million Hiroshima bombs, it blew five cubic miles of debris into the air covering an area larger than France with red-hot debris, ash and cinder. Some rocks were eight feet across. Floating chunks of pumice blocked shipping lanes 7,500 miles away. The vapour cloud rose fifty miles into the air, casting a shadow over 300,000 square miles of south-east Asia. Dust in the atmosphere turned the sun blue and the sky red as far away as Trinidad.

The tsunami washed away three hundred settlements, clearing the shores of the Sunda Strait of human habitation. Some 36,000 people were killed. A giant wave damaged river boats 2,000 miles away in Calcutta and raised the tide in the English Channel, halfway around the world.

Miraculously, the *Governor General Loudon* survived. For eighteen hours   is was cloaked in darkness by the ash cloud, unable to make progress in the hur-

ricane-force winds the eruption had unleashed. The following day she headed back to her home port of Anjer at the eastern end of the Strait, passing the tiny remnant of Krakatoa that was still visible above the sea. When she arrived, Anjer was no more.

Five months after the eruption, a researcher found spiders crawling across the island's ashy remains. Gradually vegetation returned. Then in 1927, the caldera nine hundred feet below the surface of the sea began to erupt again. In January 1928, Anak Krakatoa – Malay for Krakatoa's Child – emerged. The new cone is now over 622 feet tall and still growing.

Chile 1868

In 1868, the USS *Waterœ*, a two-masted single-stacked side-wheeler, came into the port of Arica in northern Chile. Her captain was seemingly aware of the history of the area, including a tsunami which had destroyed two Spanish galleons in Valdivia in 1575, and another which had levelled the city of Concepción in 1751.

On 8 August 1868, his vessel was moored next to a Peruvian warship and an American merchantman when an earthquake struck. On board was Lieutenant L.G. Billings who gave a startling account of what it was like to ride out a tsunami:

"I was sitting in the cabin with the captain towards four o'clock in the afternoon when we gave a sudden start. The ship was trembling with the same vibration that occurs when the anchor is let go and the chains thunder in the hawse-holes. We knew that it could be that, and we ran on deck. Our eyes were at once caught by a huge cloud of dust over the land, which was coming up from the south-east while the terrible thundering grew louder and louder. As we watched, stupefied, the hills seemed

> **"The ship made a formidable leap, and immediately afterwards we felt as though we had plunged into the abyss."**

to be capsizing, and the ground moved like a short choppy waves of a rough sea.

"The cloud swallowed up Arica. In that very instant, through its impenetrable veil, there arose shrieks for help, the din of falling houses, and the thousand mixed noises of a great calamity. Meanwhile, our ship was shaken as if by the grasp of a gigantic hand. Then the cloud passed on.

"As the dust thinned out we rubbed out eyes and stared, unable to believe what we saw: where a few seconds before there had stood a happy prosperous city, busy, active, and full of life, we saw nothing but ruins. The less seriously wounded of the unhappy people caught under the wreckage of what had been their houses were struggling among the ruins, and everywhere shrieks, cries of pain, and calls for help tore the air under the pitiless sun shining in a cloudless sky.

"We were worried about the coming of a tsumani, and we put out to sea; but the water was calm and unruffled, and it might have been supposed that the four or five minutes that we had just passed through as well as the shockingly distressing scene upon which for the moment we were turning our backs were part of a nightmare. Nevertheless, as a measure of prudence the captain set out extra anchors, had the hatches closed, the guns lashed and lifelines rigged.

"Meanwhile on shore the survivors were coming down the beach and crowding on the little jetty, calling to the crews of the ships to come and help them get their relatives out of the twisted ruins and carry them to the apparent safety of anchored vessels. This was more than we could withstand, and the yawl, with thirteen men aboard, was launched at once. It reached the shore and its crew got out, leaving only one sailor to guard the boat. We on board were in the act of organising a body of forty men to be sent ashore with axes, picks, and shovels when all at once a horse murmuring noise made us look up. Looking towards the land we saw, to our horror, that where a moment before there had been a jetty, all black with human beings, there was nothing. Everything had been swallowed in a moment by the sudden rising of the sea, which the ship, floating upon it, had not noticed. At the same time we saw the yawl and its sailor carried away by the irresistible wave towards the lofty, vertical cliff of the Morro, where they disappeared in the foam as the wave broke against the rock.

"At that very instant there was another earthquake shock, accompanied by a terrible roaring on the land that went on for several minutes. Once more we saw the ground move in waves and go from left to right, and this time the sea drew back from the land until we were stranded and the bottom of the sea was exposed, so that we saw what had never been seen before, fish struggling on the seabed and the monsters of the deep aground. The round-hulled ships rolled over on their sides, while our *Wateræ* sat down upon her flat bottom; and when the sea came back, returning not as a wave, but rather as a huge tide, it made our unhappy companions turn turtle, whereas the *Wateræ* rose unhurt on the churning water.

"From that moment on, the sea seemed to defy all natural laws. Currents rushed in opposite directions, dragging us along at a speed that we could never have reached even if we had been going at full steam. The earth was still quaking at irregular intervals, but less violently and for shorter periods each time.

"The Peruvian ironclad *America*, which as held to be one of the fastest ships in the world at the time, was still afloat, and so was the American ship *Fredonia*. The *America*, which had tried to get out to sea with her engines running at full speed before the withdrawal of the water, was nevertheless partially stranded, and her hull was stove in. Now the sea was carrying her at a great speed towards the shore, and her funnels belching thick clouds of smoke she seemed to be running in to the assistance of the helpless *Fredonia*, which was being drawn towards the cliffs of the Morro.

"we saw the ground move in waves"

Captain Dyer of the *Fredonia*, believing this to be the case, ran aft and hailed the man-of-war, which was now no more than a few yards away. 'Ahoy! You can do nothing for us, our bottom is smashed in. Save yourselves! Goodbye!' A moment later the *Fredonia* broke to pieces against the cliff and not a man was saved, while a counter-current miraculously took hold of the Peruvian ship and carried her in the other direction.

"The last rays of the sun were lighting up the Andes when we saw to our horror that the tombs in which the former inhabitants had buried their dead, in the slopes of the mountain, had opened, and in concentric rings, as in an amphitheatre, the mummies of natives dead and forgotten for centuries appeared on the surface. They had been buried sitting up, facing the sea. The nitre-impregnated soil had preserved them astonishingly, and the violent shocks that had crumbled the desert-dry earth now uncovered the horrifying city of the dead, buried long ago.

"Words cannot convey the appalling appearance of the scene. Our minds had been much worked upon by what we had undergone already and we were ready to believe that the Day of Judgement had come and that the world was going to disappear. The bitterness of so terrifying a death went beyond anything that we could imagine.

"It had been dark for some time when the lookout hailed the deck and said that a breaking wave was coming. Staring into the night we first made out a thin phosphorescent line which, like a strange kind of mirage, seemed to be rising higher and higher in the air: its crest, topped by the baleful light of that phosphorescent glitter, showed frightful masses of black water below. Heralded by the thunder of thousands of breakers all crashing together, the tidal wave that we had dreaded for hours was at last upon us.

"Of all the horrors, this seemed the worst. We were chained to the bed of the sea, powerless to escape. We had taken all the precautions that were humanly possible, and now we could do nothing but watch this monstrous wave approach, without the moral support of having something to do or the hope that the ship could go through the mass of water rushing to overwhelm us. We could only hold on to the rails and wait for the catastrophe.

"With a terrifying din, our ship was engulfed, buried under a half-liquid, half-solid mass of sand and water. We stayed under for a suffocating eternity. Then, groaning in all her timbers, our solid old *Wateræ* pushed her way to the surface, with her gasping crew still hanging on the rails. A few men were seriously hurt. None was killed and nobody was missing. It was a miracle that I can scarcely really believe in even at this length of time.

"Our survival was certainly due to the construction of the ship, her shape, and her fitting our, which allowed the water to pour off the deck almost a quickly as if she had been a raft.

"The ship had been carried along at a very great speed, but all at once she became motionless. In the end, after a short wait, we lowered the lantern over the side and we discovered that we had run aground. Where we were we could not tell. There were still a few waves that came to strike us, but they were not so strong, and presently they stopped altogether. For some time we stayed at our posts, but as the ship remained quite still and nothing further happened the order was given for the exhausted crew to go below and sleep in their hammocks.

"The sun rose upon such a spectacle of desolation as can rarely have been seen. We were high and dry, three miles from our anchorage and two miles inland. The wave had carried us at an unbelievable speed over the sand dunes which line the shore, across a valley, and beyond the railway line that goes to Bolivia, leaving us at the foot of the coastal range of the cordillera of the Andes. Upon an almost vertical cliff we found the mark that the tidal wave had left: it was forty-seven

> "Of all the horrors, this seemed the worst. "

feet up. If the wave had carried us on for another sixty yards, it would have smashed us against the perpendicular mountain wall.

"Near us there lay the wreck of the bit English three-master, the *Channaælia*; one of her anchor chains was wrapped around her as many times as its length would allow, thus showing how the vessel had rolled over and over, head over heels. Some way further off, nearer the sea, lay the ironclad *America* upon her side, quite wrecked.

"During the days that followed the earth went on shaking, but none of the tremors reach either the violence of the length of the first. Yet some were still quite strong enough to make the *Waterœ* rattle like an old kettle, and we had to leave the ship and go and camp on the plateau, two hundred feet higher up. From that height we could see the disastrous effects of the earthquake upon the topography. In some places we found enormous fissures, some of which were more than a hundred feet wide and of an unknown depth, while others were no more than ordinary cracks. Both the one kind and the other showed how panic-stricken the people must have been when they fled. For example, I remember seeing the body of a dead woman on the dead body of her horse, both having been swallowed by a crevasse as they were flying for their lives.

"The town itself had disappeared. Where it had stood there stretched an even plain of sand. Except in the suburbs on the mountain slopes there was not a single house to show where Arica had been. All the buildings, which were made of hollow bricks called abodes, have been destroyed by the shocks, and then the debris had been swept away by the sea. In the suburbs that lay above the level that the seas had reached we walked over a hideous piling up of everything, including corpses, twenty or thirty feet deep.

"Out of Arica's ten or fifteen thousand inhabitants, a bare few hundred survived. For the three long weeks during which we waited for help, we share the *Waterœ*'s victuals and drinking water with these wretched people. I will not attempt to describe our feelings when at last we saw the United States Navy frigate *Powhatan* come into the roadstead, with her holds and her decks overloaded with all possible kinds of victuals and stores."

In all, it is thought that the Chilean earthquake and tsunami of 1868 took 25,000 lives.

Japan 1854

In the Gulf of Sagami to the south of Tokyo, there is a fault. On 23 December 1854, it moved, creating a disastrous earthquake and a tsunami. This was observed by two officers on the Russian frigate *Diana*.

The officer of the watch recorded:

"We felt the first shock at 9.15 am. It was very strong and it went on for two or three minutes. At ten o'clock a huge wave rushed into the bay, and within a few minutes the whole town was underwater. The many ships at anchor were thrown against one another and seriously damaged. We immediately saw a great deal of debris floating. At the end of five minutes the water in the bay swelled and began boiling up, as if thousands of springs had suddenly broken out. The water was mixed with mud, straw and every kind of rubbish, and it hurled itself upon the town and the land to either side with shocking force. All the houses were wiped out. At 11.15 the frigate dragged her anchors and lost one of them. Presently she lost the other and the ship was then whirled around and swept along with a strength that grew greater with ever increasing speed of the water. At the same time thick clouds of vapour cover the site of the town and the air was filled with sulphurous exhalations. The rise and fall of the water in this narrow bay was such that it caused several whirlpools, among which the frigate

"The town itself had disappeared."

spun round with such force that in the midst of these gyrations, she turned clear round forty-three times, but not without sustaining serious damage. Until noon the rising up and the falling of the water in the bay did not cease. The level varied from eight to forty feet in height. Towards two o'clock the bottom of the sea rose again, and so violently that several times the frigate was laid over and the anchor was seen in no more than four feet of water. At last the sea grew calm. The frigate floated in the middle of an inextricable tangle of her own rigging and twisted chains. The bay was nothing more than an expanse of ruins."

Although ships out in the open sea rarely feel the effects of a tsunami, those at anchor in a confined body of water rarely survive. The second eyewitness's account makes it clear that the *Diana* was probably never in a condition to put to sea again:

"On the 23 December 1854, at 9.45 am, the first shock waves of the earthquake were felt on board the Russian frigate *Diana* as she lay at anchor in the harbour of Simoda, not far from Jeddo [now Tokyo], Japan. Fifteen minutes later a large wave was observed rolling into the harbour and the water on the beach to be rapidly rising. This wave was followed by another and when the two receded, which was at 10.15 am, there was not a house, save an unfinished temple, left standing in the village. These waves continued to come and go until 2.30 pm, during which time the frigate was thrown on her beam end five times. A piece of keel eighty-one feet long was torn off, holes were knocked in her by striking the bottom, and she was reduced to a wreck. In the course of five minutes the water in the harbour fell, it is said from twenty-three to three feet, and the anchors of the ship were laid bare. There was a great loss of life; many houses were washed into the sea, and many junks were carried up – one, two miles inland – and dashed to pieces on the shore. The bay was beautifully fine and no warning was given of the approaching convulsion.

It was calm in the morning and the wind continued light all day."

They were lucky not to be ashore, where over 3,000 perished.

Portugal 1775

It was around 9.40 am on the morning of All Saints' Day, 1 November 1755, and most of the devout citizens of Lisbon were in church, when an earthquake measuring 8.75 on the Richter scale

occurred somewhere out under the Atlantic Ocean.

An eyewitness heard a sound "resembling the hollow distant rumbling of thunder". The church bells began to ring on their own and the enormous chandeliers in the cathedral swang to and fro. Alarmed the worshippers ran out into the cathedral square where they met the congregation of the Church of St. Anthony. Together they prayed for deliverance. It seemed to work. The trembling stopped. Then, suddenly, a second, more destructive shock hit the city. Already weakened by the first tremor, large sections of the cathedral and St. Anthony's fell down and "buried every soul as they were standing there crowded together".

This same scene was played out across the city. In all, 17,000 out of the city's estimated 20,000 houses fell down, killing the inhabitants, and the resulting cloud of dust blocked out the sunlight.

One of the survivors was a British merchant called Braddock who was writing a letter in his apartment when they second tremor struck "with such violence that the upper storeys immediately fell, and though my apartment (which was on the first floor) did not share the same fate... it was with no small difficulty I kept my feet, and expected nothing less than to be soon crushed to death as the walls continued rocking to and fro in the frightfulest manner, opening in several large places; large stones falling down on every side from the cracks; and the ends of most of the rafters starting out from the roof. To add to this terrifying scene, the sky in a moment became so gloomy that I could now distinguish no particular object."

Fifteen minutes later a third tremor hit the city. According to Portuguese eyewitness António Pereira: "The whole tract of country about Lisbon was seen to heave like the swelling of the billows in a storm."

The fact that his disaster had taken place on All Saints' Day only made things worst. There were numerous candles in the churches, which started toppled, starting fires. A stiff north-easterly wind fanned the flames. Shopkeepers tried to salvage their stock, piling it up in the Terreiro do Paço, a riverside square, where it was consumed. The Patriarchal Church and the new opera house, which had survived the earthquake, were burnt down. In the royal library 70,000 books went up in smoke. English Protestant visitors could scarcely disguise a smirk when they learned that one of the first buildings to be burnt was the headquarters of the Inquisition, while the brothels on Suja Street remained intact.

> ## "it was with no small difficulty I kept my feet ..."

hips in the harbour at Lisboncould not survive the power of the tsunami

Braddock described the scene on the streets: "Here, mothers with infants in their arms; there, ladies richly dressed; priests, friars, gentlemen, mechanics… some had their backs or thighs broken, others had vast stones on their breasts; some lay almost buried in rubbish."

He managed to escape over the rubble and corpses to banks of the River Tagus, where he thought he would be safe. The area was filled with a frantic mob. Then, an hour after the first tremor, he heard the cry: "The sea is coming; we shall all be lost."

The sea began to ebb, then suddenly began to rise again.

"In an instant there appeared, at some small distance, a large body of water, rising as it were like a mountain," he said. "We all immediately ran for our lives, as fast as possible; many were actually swept away, and the rest about their waist in water at a good distance from the banks. For my own part, I had the narrowest escape, and should certainly have been lost had I not grasped a large beam that lay on the ground, till the water returned to its channel, which it did almost in the same instant, with equal rapidity."

Indeed he was lucky. Those that had made it to the marble quayside were swept away by a fifty-foot wave, which left not a single survivor or any trace of the vessels moored to it.

It is thought that 30,000 residents of Lisbon perished, though estimates vary from 15,000 to 75,000. The Lisbon earthquake was felt throughout the entire region. A fissure opened in a

A major trade centre, eighteenth-century Lisbon was bustling with life

coastal village in Morocco that is said to have sent its 8,000 residents tumbling into the water. Chandeliers swayed in Holland and Germany. The levels of the lakes in Switzerland and Scotland rose and fell by several feet. Sea waves caused by the earthquake were noted in England at 2 pm. Four hours later a twenty-foot wave was seen in the Lesser Antilles, on the other side of the Atlantic.

In Lisbon the aftershocks continued. The religious believed that the end of the world had come. The dying called out for absolution, while escaped galley slaves and convicts went on the rampage.

The King of Portugal had been out of Lisbon at the time of the earthquake. He returned and opened the palace kitchens to feed the survivors. His chief minister, the Marquis de Pombal, stationed troops at the gates of Lisbon to prevent the skilled workers needed to rebuild the city from leaving and to stop looters. Gallows were erected and the corpses of thirty-four looters left hanging from them to deter others.

Church approval was secured to bury the dead at sea, mitigating the threat of disease. Fire-fighting and demolition

An estimated 17,000 of the city's 20,000 houses fell down during the quake

teams went to work. The homeless were housed in temporary accommodation. Grain was requisitioned at pre-earthquake prices. Rents were fixed and no one was allowed to be thrown out of their homes. Timber was brought into the city and kilns were built at record speed to fire bricks.

Pombal realised that accurate information was needed to calm people's fears and the Gazeta de Lisboa never missed an issue. Ships were sent out to Portugal's distant empire to spread the word that Lisbon, a major trading centre, was still open for business.

The Lisbon earthquake of 1755 was one of the first to be studied scientifically. Pombal sent questionnaires out to every parish in Portugal. Italian scientists had made crude seismographs sometime before and an Englishman named John Michell published a treatise in 1760 contending that earthquakes were caused by "shifting masses of rock miles below the surface".

The destruction of Lisbon also had a literary epitaph. In Voltaire's novel *Candide*, the eponymous hero – a naif whose believes that "all is for the best in the best of all possible worlds" – having escaped the Lisbon earthquake "terrified almost out of his wits, covered with blood, and trembling violently, said to himself: 'If this is the best of all possible worlds, whatever must the others be like?'"

"terrified almost out of his wits, covered with blood ..."

Indian Ocean 2004

When the turquoise seas dramatically drained from Thailand's sun-soaked shoreline leaving fish gasping and would-be swimmers bemused, only a few recognised it as the ominous indicator of a tsunami.

They shouted warnings, ran from the beach and headed to higher ground. But there was scant time to issue alerts about the ever-rising wall of water looming on the horizon and even these well-informed witnesses could not guess at the magnitude of the impending cataclysm. Meanwhile, the vast majority had no clue about the deadly phenomena about to unfold. It was 26 December 2004, a date marking one of the world's worst natural catastrophes that changed the face of Asia and fractured the lives of the continent's coastal populations.

When the water returned it came in irresistible quantities, sweeping away everything in its path. Those who were not swiftly drowned risked injury - even impalement - in the massive amounts of debris whisked up by the waves, including hefty fishing boats and cars. It was sudden, shocking and, for hundreds of thousands of people, fatal.

Thailand was just one of many countries affected around the Indian Ocean. In Sri Lanka it was a different story, although the outcome was much the same. The sea did not vanish but swelled immediately and immensely. There were no discernible clues before its arrival and there was no mercy for the many coastal villages thronging with people. The Indian state of Tamil Nadu likewise felt the full force of the disrupted ocean.

Across the ocean in Somalia 176 people were killed and 50,000 left homeless. Even in South Africa a death was reported in Port Elizabeth and Durban harbour was closed due to the currents swirling around its mouth. Low lying 'paradise' isles, including the Maldives and the Andaman and Nicobar islands, were literally swamped.

But it was the Indonesian islands that suffered most. Two months after the tsunami bodies were still being found daily by the score. The recovery of the dead was expected to last for six months as it was these heavily populated islands lay closest to the source of the disaster.

No one will ever know the final death toll of the disaster although a figure of 310,000 is credible. Many of the dead were elderly or very young, oft-times ripped from the arms of their family by the sheer force of the water.

A tsunami – the Japanese word for harbour wave – is caused not by weather or tides but by underwater catastrophes like landslides or volcanoes. In this case, it was an earthquake off the west coast of Sumatra measuring 8.9 on the Richter scale. (Subsequent reports have put it at closer to 9.3.) It was, quite simply, one of the largest earthquakes to shake the globe in a century. A further 15 quakes followed as two of the world's 13 tectonic plates thrust against each other creating a rupture that measured 750 miles (1,200 km).

Initially, the tsunami waves that followed the tremors were shallow and moved rapidly. Only when they felt the ocean floor did the waves' height build. Sometimes a tsunami is wrongly labelled a tidal wave. In fact the tsunami 'wave

The strange swelling of the sea gave little clue of the disaster about to unfold

The devastation caused by the tsunami was eerily similar to a nuclear holocaust

train' means the affected shores are continually lashed by something that is more of a turbulent surge than a surfable wave.

In the aftermath it looked like a nuclear holocaust, with only the occasional building remaining upright. Most of the palm trees were, like homes, schools and businesses, sucked up and spat out. Beneath the tangled mess lay an unknown number of victims. Great swathes of Asia and the eastern rim of Africa turned from lush green to sludge brown in the moments it took for the water to flood inland.

The plight of the living was nightmarish for weeks afterwards. Most had lost family and continued in desperation to search for loved ones. Corpses mounted amid the rubble and debris, soon blackened and bloated beyond recognition. Food was scarce, water supplies contaminated and health care restricted or non existent. Roads were impassable, leaving the survivors of some outlying communities isolated for days.

The loss of fishing vessels meant there was no work or food for some commu-

> ... there was
> no mercy for
> the many
> coastal
> villages...

nities. The destruction of hotels kept tourists away from other areas, combining to jeopardise the economy.

As television pictures flashed across the world a humanitarian relief effort on an unprecedented scale cranked into action. Aid agencies were chiefly concerned with supplying fresh water and shelter to the grieving homeless to avert deadly epidemics and they were largely successful. However, their triumph was counterbalanced by political scraps between the government and rebel forces in both Sri Lanka and Indonesia, which hampered the distribution of supplies. In the longer term, the mental anguish suffered by survivors was inevitably acute, with many remaining inconsolable at their wide-ranging losses.

Although earthquakes cannot be predicted, tsunamis can and that is why a warning system was established in the Pacific in 1948. Before 2004 no such warning system existed in the Indian Ocean, where tsuanmis are much rarer, numbering just seven in a century. It is a shortcoming that is now being rectified.

Floods

The Yangtze River, China 1931

According to the US National Oceanic and Atmospheric Administration (NOAA), the worst flood in the history of the world occurred in August 1931 in China, when the River Yangtze over-flowed its banks. The death toll is thought to be a staggering 3.7 million from drowning, disease and starvation. In all 51million people – a quarter of the population of China – were affected.

China's then capital Nanking was flooded to a depth of three feet. An eye-witness reported that a stretch of the river 150 miles long was flood to as much as twenty miles from the bank. Thousands were washed away when the dykes burst and, already by mid-September, it was reported that a million had drowned, while others were stranded

Whole river communities have disappeared when the Yangtze bursts its banks

on little islands of higher ground, where they starved.

Tens of thousands of refugees fled to the major cities. The Times correspondent from Hankow wrote: "Imagine a mud road three miles long and fifteen yards wide, with remains of mat sheds and bits of sacking as cover. People it so thickly in your imagination that there is only a path four feet wide down the middle. Remember that about a quarter of them are children under the age of six. To this hell add pigs, chickens, ducks and emaciated dogs. Now realise that for this vast, tightly packed multitude, there are no sanitary arrangements whatsoever."

Martial law had to be declared in Hankow, with dozens of robberies taking place every night. The situation was all the more desperate because the flood had followed three years of drought.

Bangladesh

Only a quarter of Bangladesh lies more than three metres above sea level, yet more than 117 million people live there. It is regularly hit by cyclones which send storm surges up the Bay of Bengal, causing devastating floods.

In 1737, more that 300,000 drowned in the area. Since then there have been numerous efforts to build flood defences. Nevertheless over 20,000 drowned in 1963; another 40,000 in 1965. But the cyclone that hit the area in 1970 which wrecked destruction on an almost unprecedented scale.

In November 1970 a tropical cyclone with winds up to 100 miles an hour came storming up the Bay of Bengal, generating a surge of water which struck Bangladesh – then still East Pakistan – in the early hours of 13 November.

"At midnight we heard a great roar growing louder from the south east," said Kamaluddin Chodhury, a farmer on Manpura island in the Ganges Delta. "I

"It was pitch black, but in the distance I could see a glow."

looked out. It was pitch black, but in the distance I could see a glow. The glow got nearer and nearer and then I realised it was the crest of a huge wave."

Chodhury rushed his family to the roof. As the wave rolled in, Manpura Island disappeared under twenty feet of water. For five hours, the Chodhury family huddled together in the darkness, lashed by wind and rain. By dawn the waters had receded, leaving utter devastation. Chodhury's house was more solid that most. Of the 4,500 bamboo and thatch huts on the island, only four remained standing and of the island's 30,000 inhabitants, 25,000 were dead.

Across 3,000 square miles, houses were flattened and field stripped bare. Drowned bodies hung from the branches of trees or lay in heaps on beaches. In thirteen small islands off Chittagong everyone had been killed. In Bhola, the largest island in the delta, 200,000 had drowned and estimates of the total death toll range between 500,000 and a million.

The reason for the high death toll was that, three weeks earlier, there had been a cyclone warning, but the storm had fizzled out before it had hit the coast. This time, though the cyclone had been spotted by a U.S. weather satellite, the warning issued by the radio station in Dhaka was ambiguous.

The twenty-foot wave simply demolished the low earth barriers around the paddy fields. Anyone who tried to escape in the small local fishing boats was doomed. Forty-year-old rice farmer Munshi Mustander Billa survived by clinging onto a palm tree, but he saw his two daughters and three sons plucked off one by one – the youngest, a baby under one year old, was plucked from his arms. When Munshi himself was plucked from the tree, his wife, overcome with grief, let go too. But Munshi grabbed onto another tree and managed to catch hold of his wife. The water tore their clothes from their backs. They were left bedraggled and naked. And when the waters receded they had to cloth them-

The 117 million residents of Bangladesh have been blighted by flooding throughout history

selves in rags taken from corpses.

While tens of thousands of people were simply swept away, there were some remarkable tales of survival. Three days later, a wooden chest was washed ashore with six children, age three to twelve, alive inside it. Their grandfather had put them in it, then climbed in himself. But he had died of exposure.

The tales were usually of horror and pity though. One old man on Jabbar Island piled the remains of fifty-two members of his family into a single grave. Often the task of burying hundreds of thousand of corpses simply overwhelmed the survivors. In some places, they piled them on rafts and floated them out to sea. But as often as not they would be washed back to shore by the next tide.

A Red Cross airlift in to the capital Dhaka started four days later and a British warship brought more aid. But it was impossible to prevent the death toll rising from exposure, starvation and disease. A million acres of paddy fields had been swamped and seventy-five per cent of the rice crop was ruined. Most of the fishing boats were lost and a million head of cattle drowned. Destitute villagers searched the mud for single grains of rice. There was no fresh water. In urban areas the mains were broken and village springs were fouled by sea water and rotting corpses.

The government in Islamabad, West Pakistan, dragged its feet – the Punjabis there had little time for the Bengalis in the East. Forty army helicopters stood idle on the airfields of West Pakistan and it was days before the 50,000 tons of grain sitting in government warehouses were released.

Some $50 million of foreign aid put East Pakistan back on its feet again. But the survivors of the cyclone had little time for the government in West Pakistan. The following year, East Pakistan broke away and founded the independent nation of Bangladesh.

But that did not end the flooding. In 1988, sixty per cent of Bangladesh found

the task of burying hundreds of thousands of corpses simply overwhelmed the survivors.

itself underwater. The cause this time was not a tropical cyclone. Instead, the country's three great rivers, the Meghna, the Brahmaputra and the Ganges – swollen by monsoon rains – burst their banks, covering 47,000 square miles of land in under 24 hours. Water supplies became contaminated with sewage and 2,379 people died of drowning and disease. Seven million houses were flattened, leaving some thirty million homeless. Half-a-million cattle died. Two million tons of rice was destroyed and roads, railways and bridges devastated.

In April 1991, another tropical cyclone swept up the Bay of Bengal. The twenty-foot storm surge swept over low-lying areas of Bangladesh killing 140,000 and leaving millions homeless. Another hit Bangladesh in May 1997, damaging or destroying some 400,000 homes. But there had been an effective storm warning and people were able to take refuge in the cyclone shelters built after the 1991 disaster. This time only two hundred were killed.

The Yellow River, China 1887

In the past 3,000 years, since records have been kept, the Yellow River in China has flooded some 1,500 times. The reason is that, as it makes its way the 3,000 miles from Tibet, where is rises, to the Gulf of Chihli, it carries with it 1.6 billion tons of silt, making it the world's muddiest river. As the river slows when it crosses the North China Plain, it deposits this silt, constantly raising the river bottom.

Over the centuries, the Chinese authorities have tried to prevent the river flooding by building dykes along its banks. But this was only building up trouble. The river deposited its silt between the levees, raising the river bed until the river overflows. The levees constantly had to be built higher and wider until, in some places they stood eight miles back from the bank on either side.

On 28 September 1887, an old dyke wall at the bend of the river near Chengchow in Honan province cracked. At first a few feet gave way. Then the pressure of the water tore down a few hundred feet, then a few hundred yards until the whole section gave way. This slowed the river downstream of the breach, silting the river up. So there was nowhere for the water but out through the breach in the dike. Whole towns disappeared under water and silt. As least 1,500 settlements were swept away, leaving their few surviving inhabitants clinging to anything that would float. An American engineer visiting the area saw a lake the size of Lake Ontario, which covers 7,550 square miles. Somewhere between 900,000 and 2.5 million people died and further three million were missing or homeless. The survivors then suffered famine and disease.

The flood walls were repaired the following spring. But in 1935, another flood of the Yellow River killed tens of thousands and rendered millions homeless. Then in 1938, in an attempt to halt the invading Japanese, the Chinese army blew up one of the levees, drowning 500,000 of their own people.

Attempts at controlling the Yellow River began as early as the third century BC, when an engineer named Yu came up with the idea of dredging the river to encourage the water to flow in its proper channel. Yu was made Emperor of China for his efforts. Even so the situation had continued to worsen. The severe erosion upstream has not been halted and silting means that the riverbed is continuing to rise in the lower reaches. Today in some eastern sections, which are the most populous regions in China, the river bottom is higher than the surrounding plains, often by as much as three to five metres. In certain places such as Kaifeng in Henan Province, the riverbed is more than ten metres above

Whole towns disappeared under water and silt.

the city. There the bed of the river lies above the rooftops of the houses behind the levees. In such regions, the consequences would be disastrous if a dyke break occurs during the rainy season.

Dams have helped control floods, but the river's thick silt has clogged many of them. Currently the Chinese are constructing a massive new dam called the Xiaolangdi Multipurpose Dam Project. Boasting ten in-take towers, nine flood and sediment tunnels, six power tunnels and an underground powerhouse, the structure aims to finally cure "China's Sorrow".

The Yangtze River, China 1998

More than 700 small rivers join the Yangtze as it flows 4,000 miles across China and nearly half of China's 1.2 billion people live along its banks. In 1998, it flooded. There had been exceptionally high rainfall. But in the upper reaches people had cleared trees from the mountain slopes to plant crops. Without the tree roots to absorb the water, it ran straight off into the river, which overflowed its banks. Some 3,000 people were drowned and a million more left homeless. Hundreds of villages were destroyed, leaving more than fourteen million people homeless, and submerging over 54 million acres of farmland. Industries were shut down and crops were destroyed, costing the economy over $24 billion. In all 240 million people were affected.

In the Harbin and Qiqihar, and the Daqing oilfields. more than a thousand wells had to be shut down and in Tibet and south-western Yunnan province the rainfall set off landslides and mudslides that destroyed more than 700,000 homes. Shortages of grain, vegetables and other commodities in the flood-hit areas sent prices soaring. And typhoid

Any higher ground will do in the face of a flood

broke out among refugees in the north-east as flood waters spread the contents of sewers and latrines, and supplies of safe drinking water became scarce.

To this day fifteen million people and 1.6 million hectares of land along the Jingjiang section of the Yangtze River are seriously threatened by flooding. However the Chinese government have finally got around to doing something about it with their Three Gorges Dam project. As well as preventing flooding this will improve navigation on the river and provide China with massive quantities of hydro-electric power – saving the burning of around fifty million tons of coal a year. Around a million people will be relocated though and construction will affect the habitats of Chinese river dolphin and Chinese sturgeon. Artificial breeding grounds are being built and ancient monuments are being moved.

Florence, Italy 1966

Florence is the home of the Italian Renaissance and the city is crammed with priceless works of art. On 4 November 1966, the River Arno that runs through it broke its banks in what has been described as the worst artistic disaster of modern times.

It began raining on 3 November and within forty-eight hours nineteen inches had fallen – that is equivalent to four months' rainfall in two days. Over a hundred people were drowned as flood water swamped 750 villages, along with the cities of Venice, Pisa and Florence.

There were fears that the flood waters would tear down the Ponte Vecchio, the old bridge lined with goldsmiths shops that had been rebuilt after the flood of 4 November 1333, when the waters reached 13 feet 10 inches. The bridge held, but debris trapped under its arches turned it into a dam. A record twenty feet of water spilt out into the city. More

Many feared the flood would tear down the Ponte Vecchio

than six million books in the Biblioteca Nazionale were soaked. The muddy water mixed with oil and sewage left its marks on the city's frescoes, sculptures and paintings. Giovanni Cimabue's life-sized image of Christ painted in 1280 was submerged for twelve hours, losing seventy-five per cent of its pigment. The bronze panels on the doors of the baptistery at the Cathedral of Santa Maria del Fiore that marked the beginning of the Renaissance were torn off by the flood waters. But, fortunately, the railings in front of them stopped the panels from being washed away.

up to dry in the train station. Marble statues were buried in mounds of talcum powder to draw the moisture out of them. Volunteers from all over the world turned up to lend a hand. New techniques were devised to restore valuable works. Many of the frescoes were detached from the walls they had occupied for four hundred years so they could be restored in controlled conditions. Microbiologists at the University of Florence made a breakthrough in the prevention of the growth of fungus on damp plaster. And by 21 December 1966, all but one of Florence's art galleries and museums had reopened.

The works in the famous Uffizi gallery were largely saved because they were upstairs, but 130,000 photographic negatives in the basement were ruined. Other museums were not so lucky and filthy water soaked into works by Michelangelo, Donatello and other Renaissance masters. When the waters receded half-a-million tons of mud, oil, silt and sewage was left behind in the city.

The restoration work began almost immediately. Books were taken to tobacco drying sheds where each page was dried individually. Others were hung

When the River Arno burst its banks in 1966 it was described as the worst artistic disaster ever

Hurricanes

Hurricane Katrina, USA 2005

Once New Orleans was a by-word for jazz music, Mardi Gras and succulent Creole and Cajun cooking. A fortunate fusion of French, Spanish and African American influences lent the place an exotic and relaxed atmosphere. Not for nothing was it known as 'the Big Easy', originally among musicians who had no trouble finding work here until ultimately the label fitted all aspects of city life. New Orleans was also nicknamed 'the city that care forgot' and adopted an unofficial motto of 'let the good times roll'.

To live in New Orleans was to embrace this 'laissez faire' lifestyle. The only cloud on the horizon was the certain knowledge that this low-lying metropolis would be in dreadful danger if it found itself in the direct path of one of the terrible storms that lashed America's Gulf Coast during hurricane season.

At the south side of the city there is the vast Mississippi River while to the north lies Lake Pontchartrain. Keeping this massive volume of water at bay is a system of levees – long-established dykes – and canals to keep the parts of the city lying below the water level dry. If the levees were breached, the consequences for the half million inhabitants of New Orleans would be dire.

Residents knew the risk – which is why they habitually chose to bury their dead in crypts above ground rather than beneath the earth. Meanwhile expert analysts occasionally made their fears known. A feature in *Civil Engineering Magazine* as recently as June 2003 by J J Westerink warned that some of the levees were 'rudimentary' and insuffi-

Inside the Superdome, traumatized people grew accustomed to the notion they were at the bottom of the pile for assistance.

cient for the task. Yet still nothing significant was done by the relevant authorities to improve those defences.

So the disaster that began unfolding on 29 August 2005 had a sour taste of inevitability. Hurricane Katrina, a frenzy of high winds and rain, was following a path that led close to New Orleans. Its strength flirted with high level category five, when a number of the levees were only designed to stand up to a category three. Those alert to weather warnings with a car and sufficient cash joined the traffic jam that led out of the city. A frighteningly large number, however, had no option but to stay home and endure the storm.

Hopes that New Orleans would miss the worst effects of Hurricane Katrina at the expense of other areas, including Louisiana state capital Baton Rouge, were dashed when storm surges burst through several levees, emptying the waters of canals leading from Lake Pontchartrain into the streets. Now thousands of residents who stayed put were in peril as the waters rose above first and then second floor levels, forcing them into attics or onto rooftops. Their plight was compounded by the loss of electricity and telephone networks – and the sight of bloated corpses bobbing about below. Polluted waters lapped around the survivors' submerging perches where they were without food or fresh water, at risk of fire, dehydration and disease. Their only hope was that a passing boat or helicopter would spot their plight and rescue them. The horror went on street after street, covering neighbourhoods city-wide.

Initially the authorities appeared transfixed by the sheer scale of the disaster. As the world watched on television the emotional pleas for help made by homeless, starving and thirsty victims,

When the levee breaks: flood defences outside New Orleans are overwhelmed by the rains of Katrina

there was little evidence of an orchestrated aid effort. Nowhere was this more starkly apparent than at the Superdome football stadium, which had become a beacon for some 25,000 refugees. There they expected to find supplies and shelter while they awaited evacuation. They discovered food and drink were short, the sanitary conditions were woeful while the pledge to supply fleets of buses on which to escape the mayhem was broken day after day. Inside, traumatized people who had already suffered the destruction of their worldly possessions grew accustomed to the notion they were nevertheless at the bottom of the pile for assistance. The bodies of a few too frail to survive the ordeal were covered with ill-fitting blankets and pushed to the wall.

Suspicions that the muted response by the authorities was because the victims were largely poor and black rather than wealthy and white were soon being voiced around the world.

Tales of lawlessness both at the Superdome and outside became common currency. News of murder and rape – even of babies – was flashed across the world while scenes of looting were relayed by the media. Much later it became clear that the stories were grossly exaggerated or even made up. Looting had indeed taken place but no distinction was made between those carting off white goods – regardless of flood damage – and those fishing grocery supplies out of the murky waters because they were parched and famished and

Fire and Water: A fireman helps a man out of flood waters as a home burns in New Orleans

nothing else had been offered to them.

However, New Orleans already had a reputation for violence. Perhaps with this in mind President George Bush ordered the National Guard on to the streets in numbers to protect empty, wrecked businesses while close by people remained trapped and bodies of the dead were left uncollected.

A week after the catastrophe Mayor Ray Nagin ordered the evacuation of the city to prevent a myriad of infections from taking root. Even now, though, there were residents who refused to co-operate, notably those who would have been compelled to leave beloved pets behind. Once again reality seemed at odds with the official line. Political fallout following widespread criticism of the state and federal responses to Katrina began when the mopping up operation was still in its infancy.

Thousands of body bags were delivered to the city in the wake of Katrina. The surprising news was that, after body retrieval began some 10 days after the disaster, the death toll was less than expected. Just over a thousand people

died throughout Louisiana because of Katrina and a further 228 perished in Mississippi. There were 14 deaths in Florida and two each in Alabama and Georgia.

The most encouraging aspect of the disaster was the way Americans across the 52 states offered their homes and funds to New Orleanians left destitute.

It was days before the pumps frequently used to clear the city of water but swamped in the storm were repaired and back in action. Happily it took much less time than predicted to clear the submerged city of the grey, stinking waters that drowned its streets – despite the arrival of subsequent hurricanes. Within two weeks people began to return, initially to salvage their belongings and later to rebuild their lives. Alas, the oil rigs overturned in the hurricane in the nearby Gulf would take longer to put right than the water levels, inflicting painful price rises on an American public still reeling with shock at the natural disaster that engulfed a cherished corner of the union and exposed painful political sores that would take years to heal.

Galveston, USA 1900

On 4 September 1900, the US Weather Bureau issued a storm warning. A "tropical storm disturbance moving northward over Cuba" was thought to be heading for Florida. Two days later, it hit, causing extensive flooding. Then it veered to the west, out over the open waters of the Gulf.

At 10.30 am on 7 September, Isaac Cline, director of the weather station at Galveston, Texas, received an message from Washington to hoist storm-warning flags. The wind was blowing at just seventeen miles an hour and most Galvestonians took no notice, while vacationers packed the beaches. Most enjoyed the cool breeze from the sea after the stifling weather of the last few days. The barometer was falling, but the sky remained clear and a reporter for the *Galveston News* wrote that the storm had "changed its course or spent its force before reaching Texas" for publication in the next morning's edition. He could not have been more wrong.

Isaac Cline's brother Joseph, who was chief clerk of the weather station, woke at 4 am to find water in the back yard. That meant that the tide had risen five feet above normal. Joseph returned to the weather station, while Isaac roused the neighbours. A few had the good sense to leave their homes and head for higher ground. But most were not alarmed. Galveston was built on a sand bar and flooded frequently.

At 8.45 am it began to rain and Joseph Cline received a message from Washington that the storm had changed direction from north-west to north-east. But when he went to change the storm-warning flags he found they had been ripped from the flag staff.

By noon people were being lashed with rain as they belatedly headed for higher ground, only to find that the causeways connecting Galveston to the mainland

By noon people were being lashed with rain as they belatedly headed for higher ground.

It is estimated that some 6,000 people died in Galveston.

had been washed away. By 2.30 pm, the weather station's rain gauge had been blown away. Joseph tried to send a message to Washington only to find that the telegraph lines were down. He managed to send a wire to Houston. Soon after, that line went down too and Galveston was cut off from the outside world.

By 5.30 pm, the weather station's wind gauge had been blown away, after registering wind speeds of over a hundred miles an hour. Slate tiles torn from the city's roofs were flying through the air with enough force to take a person's head off. The barometer was still dropping and weaker structures were blown down by the high winds. Fifty neighbours took refuge in the Clines' house, which was considered one of the strongest around. Another thousand packed into the Tremont Hotel, which was built on one of the highest points of the city. By 6 pm, the front desk was underwater. The wind was gusting to an estimated 120 miles an hour and buildings were being literally blown away.

At 6.30 pm, the city was then hit by a four-foot storm surge, which demolished most of the remaining houses, killing those inside. The Clines' house was hit by a streetcar trestle carried on the surge which knocked the house over. Isaac and Joseph managed to grab Isaac's three young daughters, but Isaac's wife and most of those taking refuge in the house were carried away. The Cline brothers and the three girls eventually reached safety by clambering from one pile of floating debris to the next.

At 10 pm, the hurricane's vortex hit. By that time the sea level in the city was 15.2 feet above the high-tide mark. The wind then turned to the south. Its force dropped, but the ebbing water still had enough strength to rip buildings from their foundations and carry them out into the Gulf.

It is estimated that some 6,000 Galvestonians died in the storm, along with another 4,000 to 6,000 along the Texas coast. And some $20-million-

A traditional woodcut showing the devastation of the Galveston storm

worth of property damaged – $400 million at today's prices – was done. Hundreds of people died when a church they had taken refuge in collapsed on top of them. More than a hundred patients died in a city hospital and eighty-seven of the ninety children at St Mary's Orphanage perished. One child was saved when its parents nailed it through the wrists to the roof of their house and a woman was washed out to sea in a wooden bath-tub to be returned safely on the next morning's tide.

Martial law was declared and six looters were shot on sight. One reportedly had twenty-three severed ring-fingers in his pocket.

In 1904 a three-mile defensive wall

was built along the sea front at Galveston. It has since been extended to ten miles. Behind it, the city was raised by as much as seventeen feet in places. Some 2,156 buildings, including St Patrick's Church – weighing 3,000 tons – had to be jacked up, then the 500-block area was filled with millions of tons of sand.

Typhoon Vera, Japan 1958

On 26 September 1959, Typhoon Vera struck Honshu, the largest of Japan's islands, with winds of up to 160 miles an hour. But no one panicked. Three or four typhoons strike Japan every year. There had been five days warning. While flights in and out of the area were can-

celled, the inhabitants simply put up storm shutters, got in extra food and water, and waited.

As it happened, Nagoya, Japan's third-largest city with a population of 1.3 million, lay directly in the typhoon's path. It struck late on Saturday night when the tide was full. A wall of water seventeen feet high crashed into the city, battering the seawalls and dykes with a force of up to six tons per square foot. Any building that was standing in its way was levelled.

The city flooded. Winds tore the roofs off houses and hurled deadly debris across the city. Twenty-one ships were beached – seven of them ocean-going vessels. Logs from lumberyards battered buildings. One block collapsed trapping eighty-four people in the wreckage.

Within three hours the typhoon had moved on, leaving Nagoya flooded and full of dead bodies. No help came from Tokyo as it had also been hit by Vera.

US Navy ships made food drops to survivors

Households were literally moved by Typhoon Vera

The survivors were soon starving. Some resorted to eating scraps of food floating in the polluted waters which gave then dysentery.

Fifty school children attracted the attention of a passing helicopter, by forming the Japanese character for "help" on a nearby hill. The US Navy rode to the rescue dropping food and other supplies. But a week after Vera had struck, 25,000 hungry people were still marooned on their rooftops.

Vera's death toll was 5,000, though hundreds more had been swept away and were never found. Another 32,285 were injured. Forty thousand homes were destroyed, leaving 1.5 million people homeless, and 510,000 acres of farmland were devastated. In all, over $2 billion-worth of damaged had been done.

Hurricane Mitch, Central America 1998

On 21 October 1998, a tropical depression formed in the southern Caribbean Sea. The following day, it was given the name Mitch. Over the next five days, Mitch strengthened from a tropical storm to a category five hurricane.

Mitch continued to gather strength as it moved to the north-west. Its winds reached a peak of 157 knots, or 180 miles an hour, on 26 October as it reached the north-east coast of Honduras, making Mitch the strongest hurricane in the Caribbean in a decade and the fourth strongest ever seen in the Atlantic basin.

By the morning of 28 October, the

Then Mitch stalled and the rains increased ...

winds had dropped to 105 knots. Now moving more slowly, it caused heavy rain over Honduras and Nicaragua. Then Mitch stalled and the rains increased, causing catastrophic flooding and mudslides. Mitch weakened when it made landfall on 29 October but the mountains of Central America continued to "squeeze" the moisture out of it.

Mitch then moved to the north. Emerging over the warm waters of the Gulf of Mexico, it began to pick up speed again. On 4 November, Mitch hit the west coast of Florida with winds still gusting to nearly seventy knots. Hardest hit were the Florida Keys, where tornadoes flipped mobile homes, felled trees and snapped power lines. Only six weeks before Hurricane Georges had destroyed or damaged four thousand homes along the 120-mile island chain.

Mitch also hit south and central Florida. Some 7.5 inches of rain flooded streets in Miami and tornadoes damaged houses. The Bahamas were lashed with high winds and rains before the storm eventually broke up a hundred miles to the north of the islands. But Mitch's most lethal legacy had been left in Central America, where it is believed 11,000 died, many swept away in torrents that overcame flood defences that had been standing for 200 years.

Hurricane Mitch made its appearance during the 1998 Atlantic hurricane season, which was the deadliest in more than two hundred years. Not since the Great Hurricane struck Barbados and Martinique in 1780 has the Atlantic region seen so many storm-related fatalities. In 1998 there were fourteen tropical storms of which ten became hurricanes. Three of these became major hurricanes of categories three, four and five. And in the four-year period 1995-1998 there were a total of thirty-three hurricanes, an all-time record.

Popular resorts in the Gulf of Mexico were evacuated in the face of the hurricane's onslaught

Nothing could stand in the face of Mitch's 180mph winds

Hurricane Mitch overcame flood defences that had stood for 200 years

Air Disasters

Tenerife was the world's worst-ever air disaster

Tenerife 1977

The world's worst aeroplane disaster took place on the ground at Rodeos Airport on Tenerife in the Canary Islands on 27 March 1977 when two Boeing 747s collided on the runway. A KLM jet was speeding down the fog-bound runway to take-off and ran into a Pan Am plane, on charter from Los Angeles, which was taxiing into position.

All 248 passengers and crew on board the KLM jumbo were killed instantly, along with 326 people on the Pan Am plane. 70 survived the initial crash, but the death toll eventually climbed to 583.

It is thought that the accident was caused by a misunderstanding in the use of English. The KLM pilots misunderstood what the air traffic controller had said and thought he had been given clearance to take off. A similar misunderstanding caused a crash in New York in January 1990, when an Avianca Boeing 707 en route from Medellin in Colombia to New York's JFK airport was put into a holding pattern while awaiting permission to land. The plane was low on fuel but the crew was unable to communicate the urgency of the low fuel situation to air traffic control. Due to bad weather the crew had to abort an attempted landing and soon afterwards

Only fragments of the two planes are recognisable

fuel ran out. The plane crashed into woods killing seventy-three out of the 158 passengers and crew. And in Cali, Colombia in December 1995, an American Airlines plane, travelling from Miami, crashed into a mountain while descending, killing 163 passengers and crew. The air traffic controller told

Amazingly 70 people survived the initial crash

One jet engine sits remarkably unscathed amongst the carnage

investigators he knew information given by the flight crew was inconsistent with the instructions he had issued. However the controller and crew shared no common language, he could not seek clarification from the pilot.

In December 2001 the International Civil Aviation Organisation, the UN body responsible for setting safety standards for air transport, accepted proposals to standardise the English used for communication between pilots and air traffic controllers in an attempt to end this sort of confusion. But the new rules are not likely to be adopted by the organisation's 187 member states until 2008 at the earliest – and then only after protracted negotiations with countries hostile to attempts to impose English on them at the expense of their own languages.

In the meantime, a crash claimed more than 110 lives in Milan in an accident that bears a chilling resemblance to the

> **By the time the SAS jet managed to swerve, a collision was unavoidable.**

1977 disaster in Tenerife. On 8 October 2001, a SAS jet took off while a German Cessna was taxiing on the runway in thick fog and Milan airport's ground radar system was out of action. The SAS pilot was accelerating towards take-off when the Cessna suddenly loomed out of the fog. He appears to have swerved at the last minute, but by then a collision was unavoidable. Both planes were wrecked and scores of people died.

Antarctica 1979

At 8.20 am on 28 November 1979, Flight 901 left Auckland Airport in New Zealand on an eleven-hour return sightseeing flight over Antarctica. There were 237 passengers and twenty crew aboard.

Captain Jim Collins and his co-pilot Greg Cassin had not flown over the

Antarctic before, but the DC-10's computerised navigation system was programmed to keep the plane on course. Unknown to them two of the longitude and latitude co-ordinates had been changed, moving the flight path of the aircraft thirty miles to the east.

Once over the Antarctic, Collins flew low to give his passengers a better view. But Flight 901 was not flying across the flat ground of McMurdo Sound, as he thought, but across Lewis Sound towards Mount Erebus, a 12,500 foot

high active volcano. And the snow-covered mountain was not visible against the white background of Antarctic ice.

At 12.49 pm the deck altitude alarm sounded, but there was no time for the pilots to react. Six seconds later Flight 901 hit the side of Mount Erebus and disintegrated.

The wreckage left a 2,000-foot trail across the lower slopes of Mount Erebus. The fuel tanks exploded and a fireball ripped through what was left of the fuselage. All 257 people on board had

An internal and external view of a DC-10 similar to flight 901

died and the plane was so far off its flight path that it took a rescue party twenty hours to find it.

The task of recovering and identifying the bodies of the passengers and crew was made more difficult because of the numbers involved. Over sixty people worked on the accident site, most in body recovery. On board there were New Zealanders, twenty-four Japanese, twenty-two Americans, six British, two Canadians, one Australian, one Frenchman and one Swiss. In all, 213 victims were eventually identified, but forty-four were mutilated beyond recognition.

Early in the investigation into the causes of the disaster, it became clear that there was no mechanical reason for the crash. The flight recorder tapes showed there had been no emergency in the cockpit of the aircraft. The commission of inquiry placed the blame on the pilots' inexperience and the airline systems that had allowed the aircraft to be programmed to fly on the path which led directly to Mount Erebus.

A wooden cross was erected above Scott Base to commemorate the disaster. In 1986 it was replaced with an aluminium cross after the original one was eroded by ice and snow. The Mount Erebus disaster remains New Zealand's biggest single tragedy, with one more death than in the Napier Earthquake of 1931.

Chicago 1979

On 25 May 1979 an American Airlines DC-10 took off from O'Hare International Airport in Chicago. The plane reached a height of 400 feet before the thrust of take-off tore the left-hand engine off the wing. The resulting crash killed all 271 people on board the plane and two persons on the ground. It was the worst air accident in United States history.

... forty-four were mutilated beyond recognition.

American Airlines Flight #191 was on its way to Los Angeles and was filled to near capacity as it was the start of the Memorial Day weekend. Among those on board were Playboy magazine's managing editor Sheldon Wax, his wife, author Judith Wax, and the magazine's fiction editor, Vicki Haider.

Soon after 3 pm Central Standard Time, the DC-10 was cleared by O'Hare tower for takeoff. The plane carried a heavy load of jet fuel for its 1,700-mile flight. It thundered down the runway and lifted off. But the moment it took to the air, the port engine fell from the wing. It plummeted to the ground, skidded to the end of the runway and came to a rest in some dirt.

With one engine missing, the plane was in desperate trouble and it began to roll sharply to the left. The control tower radioed the captain Walter Lux and asked if he wanted clearance for an emergency landing. There was no response. Less than a minute after takeoff, the plane smashed into the ground and caught fire about a half mile from the end of the runway. The inferno was so intense that firefighters and rescue personnel could not get near it and the flames and smoke from the wreckage reached twice the height of the plane at its highest.

Crash investigators from the National Transportation Safety Board pieced together hundreds of pieces of the wreckage and concluded that factors contributing to the cause of the accident included "the vulnerability of the design of the pylon attach points to maintenance damage; the vulnerability of the design of the leading edge slat system to the damage which produced asymmetry; deficiencies in Federal Aviation Administration surveillance and reporting systems which failed to detect the use of improper maintenance procedures; deficiencies in the practices and communications among operators, the manufacturer, and the FAA which failed to determine or disseminate the particulars regarding previous maintenance damage incidents; and the intolerance of prescribed operational procedures to this unique emergency".

Experts agreed that it was impossible to control the plane once an engine has fallen off, especially during take-off. No blame was attached to the pilots as there was no possibility they could have recovered the situation.

After the crash, all DC-10s were grounded and inspections found weaknesses in the engine mounts on other planes that could have had similar catastrophic results.

Paris 1974

Three hundred and forty six people died needlessly on 3 March 1974, when a McDonnell Douglas DC-10 operated by Turkish Airlines crashed into a forest outside Paris. The cargo door had not been properly closed, and as the plane

The collapsed floor had jammed the control lines ...

gained altitude, the door blew off. As the cargo compartment decompressed, the floor above gave way. Six passengers still strapped to their seats were sucked out of the gaping hole to their deaths.

The remaining passengers had only a few seconds more to live. The collapsed floor had jammed the control lines to the tail, making it impossible to fly the plane. Seventy-two seconds after the cargo door had blown off, the plane crashed, killing everyone on board.

It need never have happened. Two years before the cargo door had blown off an American Airlines DC-10 flying from Detroit to Buffalo, but Captain Bryce McCormick and First Officer Peter Witney had managed to land the stricken aircraft safely. On that occasion, the only "casualty" was a corpse in a coffin which had been sucked out of the open door and dropped unceremoniously from a great height.

At the enquiry into the incident, a loader had revealed that he had had trouble closing the cargo doors on the

Paris was in shock in the wake of the accident

DC-10. Little had been done to rectify this problem before the Paris crash in 1974.

New Delhi 1996

At 6.30 pm on 12 November 1996, just as the sun was setting, a Saudia 747 with 312 passengers aboard took off from New Delhi's Indira Ghandi International Airport, heading for Saudi Arabia. Seven minutes later, it was cleared to climb to 14,000 feet. Meanwhile a Kazakh Ilyushin Il-76 cargo plane with thirty-eight on board was authorised to descend to 15,000 feet on its final approach to the airport. Then suddenly, the radar blips of the two aircraft disappeared from the air traffic controllers' radar screens.

In cloudy skies some sixty miles to the west of New Delhi, the two planes had collided, creating giant fireballs that turned the sky red. The pilot of a US Air Force transport plane carrying supplies for the American Embassy in New Delhi witnessed the crash from 20,000 feet.

"We noticed out of our right-hand (side of the plane) a large cloud lit up with an orange glow, from within the clouds," he said. "The glow intensity of the cloud became dimmer and the two fireballs descended and became fireballs on the ground."

Wreckage, baggage and body parts were scattered across six miles of wheat and mustard fields near the town of Charkhi Dadri. The first people to arrive at the scene said the air was filled with the smell of burning flesh.

One of them, nineteen-year-old college student Manjit Singh, saw sixty or seventy bodies, but said that only about fifteen were identifiable. The faces of the rest were horribly charred and disfigured. Some 200 bodies were collected from the fields. Nothing remained of the other 150 people on board.

A similar accident occurred over

... body parts were scattered across six miles...

southern Germany on 2 July 2002 when another Russian Tupolev 154 airliner carrying ninety-five people collided with a Boeing 757 cargo aircraft operated by the courier company DHL and carrying a crew of three. The crash occurred shortly before midnight at 35,000 feet above the state of Baden-Württemberg.

Witnesses described seeing two large balls of flames fall from the sky and wreckage from the crash was spread over a twenty-five-mile area.

"I saw the planes hit," said one witness. "There was a huge orange fireball. There are bodies on the ground across this massive slaughter field. People are looking on simply shocked. They are searching with spotlights, looking through a field of death. It seems a hopeless task."

Another eyewitness witness told reporters: "I saw a flash of light so enormous that it lit up everything."

Police radio reported that bodies were lying everywhere. Police switchboards were jammed with calls about the crash and emergency services from across southern Germany were called in.

A farm, a school and several houses near the town of Überlingen on the banks of Lake Constance, close to the Swiss and Austrian borders, were set on fire by the falling debris. Two bodies were found among the debris on a road in the village of Owingen on the Bodensee, the resort area of Lake Constance. Other bodies fell into the lake itself.

The Tupolev was flying from Moscow to Barcelona, while the Boeing was flying from Bergamo in Italy to Brussels. They were under the control of Swiss air traffic control at the time of the accident.

Tupolev 154s have a bad record. In 1994, an Aeroflot Tupolev crashed in Russia, killing 120 people. A China Northwest Airlines Tupolev crashed in China later that year killing all 160 passengers on board. More than 140 died in July 2001 when a Tupolev 154 burst into flames and crashed near Irkutsk in Siberia. And in October that year a

Tupolev exploded in mid-air over the Black Sea while flying from Tel Aviv to Siberia, killing all seventy-six on board. It later emerged that it had been shot down accidentally by Ukrainian forces carrying out a live missile firing exercise.

By contrast, the Boeing 757 has an excellent safety record, although two of the aircraft hijacked and crashed on 9/11 were 757s.

Kinshasa 1996

At least 250 people were killed when a cargo plane crashed into a crowded street market in Kinshasa, capital of Zaire (now the Democratic Republic of the Congo), and burst into flames. Most of the victims were women and children shopping at the market.

The Antonov 32 cargo plane simply failed to get airborne. Witnesses said it got only a few feet off the ground before crashing. It continued on the ground straight across the street at the end of the runway into the market which was a shanty town made from wood and corrugated iron. The plane ploughed on through the market for about a hundred yards before coming to a halt, leaving a trail of mutilated bodies in its wake. A fire crew from the airport rushed to the scene to fight the flames. Between forty and sixty injured people were treated at the scene, but rescue efforts were hampered by people who descended on the downtown airport in search of their relatives.

The four Russian crew members, who survived the crash, were arrested.

It is thought that the plane had failed to get airborne because it was overloaded. The previous month an overloaded Lockheed Electra passenger plane owned by a private Zairean firm crashed in Angola killing 141 people, but there were few regulations in Zaire to prevent such disasters occurring. However, after years of civil war and

neglect, leaving the road network in Zaire a shambles, hundreds of small private airline companies have sprung up, providing the only viable means of transportation in the vast African country.

Long Island 1996

A Trans World Airlines jumbo jet bound for Paris on 17 July 1996 crashed into the Atlantic Ocean about a half hour after leaving Kennedy Airport in New York. All 230 people on board flight TWA 800 were killed in the crash. They included sixteen members of a high school French club and five chaperons from Montoursville, Pennsylvania.

Witnesses described seeing two explosions, and then a bright red fireball falling into the ocean. The plane appeared to break into two pieces before disappearing into the sea.

At first, federal officials thought the crash had been caused by a bomb, although they found no evidence for this. They also looked into the possibility that the plane had been struck by a missile as an unexplained blip appeared on radar screens just before the crash and witnesses had seen a streak of light moving toward the plane. But the plane was flying too high to be hit by conventional ground-to-air missiles.

National Transportation Safety Board Vice Chairman Robert Francis concluded that "there is no evidence at this point that this is not an accident". The most likely explanation was that a catastrophic mechanical failure had ignited the 250,000 pounds of fuel on the plane. A ValuJet plane crash in Florida two months earlier was believed to have been caused by a fire in the plane's cargo hold.

However, in September 2000 a new theory was put forward. It was suggested that TWA 800 was downed by electromagnetic pulses from military craft, which may have been responsible for

An unexplained blip appeared on radar screens...

several civilian airline disasters. Crash investigators had noted similarities between several tragedies. In particular, they noticed a long list of common features in the crash of TWA 800 on 17 July 1996 and the downing of Swissair 111 on 2 September 1998.

Both planes took off from New York's JFK. Both crashes occurred on a Wednesday. And both flights took off at exactly the same time, 8.19 pm. They both took the same route over Long Island and both reported trouble in the same region of airspace. Both planes crashed after suffering catastrophic electrical malfunctions. And on both occasions the planes were flying at a time when extensive military exercises involving submarines and US Navy P3 fighter planes were being conducted.

It has been suggested that strong electromagnetic pulses generated by military machinery may have triggered short-circuits in the two planes. In TWA 800, a short-circuit could have caused a spark, igniting a fire in the fuel tanks. Or a pulse could have knocked out instruments, causing the Boeing 747 to spin out of control. In the case of the Swissair 111, a fire was reported in the cabin, before the plane plunged into the sea off the coast of Nova Scotia.

Concorde 2000

At 4.42 pm on 25 July 2000, Concorde Flight AF4590 was cleared for take off at Charles de Gaulle airport in Paris. One minute and 13 seconds later, the control tower radioed the crew the alarming message: "You have flames, you have flames behind you." But the crew could do nothing to fight the devastating fire.

The pilots had already detected a problem with engine two under the left wing and shut it down. They made a desperate attempt to gain height while the control tower cleared Concorde to make an emergency landing at nearby Le Bourget airport. But, with airspeed warnings and fire alarms sounding in the background, pilot Christian Marty said simply: "Too late...no time."

Eyewitnesses reported seeing a fireball

Concorde crashed minutes after take-off, flames trailing behind the aircraft

"You have flames, you have flames behind you."

Flames trail behind the stricken aircraft in this dramatic newsreel still photo

trailing from an engine on the aircraft's left-side, and that it was not able to gain sufficient altitude before it crashed.

Seconds later, the plane hit the ground near the town of Gonesse, ploughing through a small hotel. There was a huge ball of fire and an enormous plume of black smoke. Within minutes of the crash, dozens of fire engines and ambulances raced to the scene to tackle the blaze and search for survivors. But all 109 passengers and crew were killed, along with four people on the ground.

Sections of the Relais Bleu hotel had been reduced to burning rubble and twisted metal. The blackened hulk of the Concorde was barely recognisable. The Air France plane had been chartered by a German tour operator to take German tourists to New York to join a cruise ship bound for Ecuador.

A metal strip on the runway, which had fallen off a Continental Airlines DC-10, had burst one of the plane's tyres. Parts of the burst tyre hit the wing, puncturing a fuel tank and the leaking fuel caught fire. Unable to retract the undercarriage and with both engines one and two out of action, the pilots found it impossible to gain height, making the crash inevitable. It was the first crash in Concorde's twenty-four-years of service.

However tyre bursts have been a regular problem for Concorde. A bad landing blew out a plane's tyre in 1979. The incident led to a design modification. And in 1993 a blow-out threw off a water deflector which pierced the fuel tank on a British Airways plane while taxiing. After that, the Air Accident Investigation Branch recommended changes. BA carried out modifications to the wheel apparatus, but Air France did not.

The Paris crash came one day after British Airways confirmed hairline cracks had been discovered in the wings of all seven of its Concorde fleet. However, the Paris crash had nothing to do with these cracks. The Air France plane had been inspected a few days before and given a clean bill of health.

After the Paris crash, British Airways and Air France grounded their fleet of Concordes. After extensive modifications, strengthening the tyres and adding a protective liner to the fuel tank, they went back into service. But the disaster had shaken passengers' confidence in the plane and by 2003 it proved uneconomical to keep the planes flying.

Passengers had to surrender all matches and cigarette lighters.

The Hindenburg 1937

The *Hindenburg* was the largest rigid airship ever built. At 804 feet long, it was roughly the length of three jumbo jets parked end to end. The *Hindenburg* was the sister ship to the already famous *Graf Zeppelin II*, and was launched at Friedrichshafen in Germany in 1936. It was named after Paul Hindenburg, World War I military leader and now President of Germany.

The German Zeppelin company was the leading builder of airships and aimed to challenge the supremacy of the passenger liners on the North Atlantic. With a top speed of eighty-four miles an hour, the *Hindenburg* could make the

The Hindenburg could make a transatlantic trip in just 65 hours

transatlantic trip in just sixty-five hours. It offered the same luxury as a liner. Each of the twenty-five double cabins had hot and cold running water and the airship had its own bar. Even though the airship was lifted by explosively flammable hydrogen, the *Hindenburg* had a smoking room, which was protected by a system of double doors. The only lighter on board was chained to the side of the

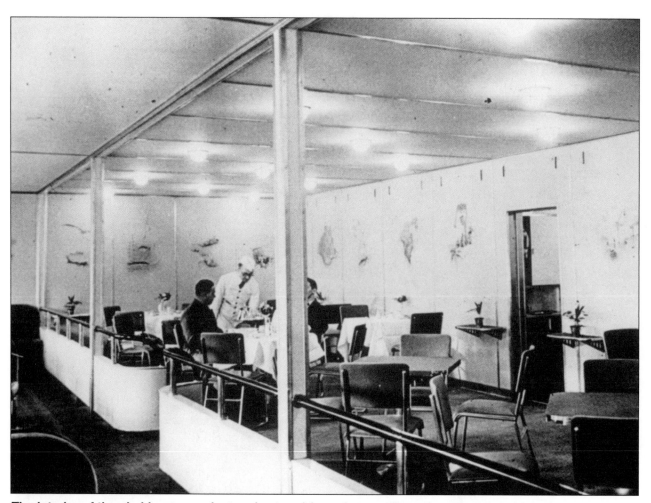

The interior of the airship was opulent and catered for only a small number of passengers

room. Passengers had to surrender all matches and cigarette lighters when boarding.

Instead of using hydrogen, the designers had wanted to use the non-flammable gas helium, but Adolf Hitler was already in power in Germany and the US, who had the only significant stock of the inert gas, feared that airships might be used for military purposes if Germany had access to helium. However, hydrogen-filled German airships had proved safe enough, crossing the Atlantic regularly without mishap since 1928.

The *Hindenburg* herself had already carried 1,002 passengers safely on ten round trips between Germany and the US when she left Frankfurt with thirty-six passengers and sixty-one crew on 4 May 1937. On this occasion the flight had been delayed because of storms at Lakehurst, the naval air station that served as an airship terminal in New Jersey. Nevertheless, the *Hindenburg* made good time over the Atlantic and at around 7 pm on 6 May 1937, she arrived at Lakehurst and nuzzled into position beside her mooring mast. At 7.25, mooring ropes were thrown down to the ground crew and the engines were reversed for braking. Suddenly a huge flame shot out of the top of the *Hindenburg*. The huge airship then crashed to the ground and was consumed by the flames in little under a minute.

Of the ninety-seven passengers and crew on board, thirty-five died, along with one member of the ground crew.

A number of theories have been advanced to explain the spectacular demise of the *Hindenburg*. Most recently, it has been stated that it was the covering of the skin of the *Hindenburg*, rather than the hydrogen, which caught fire and burned so fiercely. The skin was coated with a substance containing iron

Many claimed the explosion was the work of anti-Nazi saboteurs

oxide and an aluminium acetate, both of which are highly flammable. This theory seems unlikely, however, given the high speed of the conflagration, and a more likely theory is that a snapped staywire had pierced the skin and static electricity had ignited the escaping gas. Almost inevitably, there were mutterings of anti-Nazi sabotage, particularly from Hugo Eckener, a former head of the Zeppelin company. The *Hindenburg* was a highly-visible prestige symbol of the Nazi regime, and was marked prominently with Nazi swastikas. No evidence was ever produced to support this view, however.

Although Germany continued to build airships after the *Hindenburg* tragedy, the US continued to refuse to supply helium. Public confidence in airships was destroyed and with the coming of World War II in 1939, the remaining airships were broken up and their aluminium airframes used to make warplanes.

The Hindenburg was marked prominently with Nazi swastikas.

A huge flame shot out of the top of the Hindenburg as it moored in Lakehurst

Japan 1985

On 13 August 1985, a Japanese Air Lines jumbo jet crashed into a mountain range, killing 517 passengers and crew, and making the accident the worst air crash involving a single plane.

Miraculously there were three survivors. More could have been saved as they heard the groans of other survivors. One even heard the cries of their father and sister who later perished. The plane had crashed at about 7 pm, just after it got dark. But the Japanese rescue workers did not arrive on the scene until dawn the following morning because neither the civilian nor military rescue workers had night rescue equipment.

US military rescue teams at an American airbase less than half-an-hour away had the necessary night rescue equipment, which had been developed during the Vietnam War. American authorities informed the Japanese government that they had the equipment and the men sat up all night waiting for the call. But the US offer of help was not accepted – as a result of Japanese national pride, it is thought.

The crash led to a ground-breaking court case. On board was Akihisa Yukawa, a wealthy executive of Sumitomo Bank. While his two legitimate sons received £900,000 compensation from JAL and Boeing, his illegitimate daughter fifteen-year-old violin prodigy Diana Yukawa and her sister seventeen-year-old Cassie, a talented pianist, were offered scholarships worth less that £300 a month. The sisters sued so that they could continue their studies at the Royal College of Music.

Using DNA testing to prove their relationship to the dead banker, they won a ruling in a British Court. However, the case has yet to pass to the courts in Japan, where illegitimacy is still considered a source of shame.

Rescue workers did not arrive on the scene until the morning after the crash

Shipwrecks

Halfiax was Canada's major wartime port

Mont Blanc 1917

On 6 December 1917, the Norwegian vessel *Imo* ran into the *Mont Blanc*, a French freighter loaded with 5,000 tons of explosives, in the harbour at Halifax, Nova Scotia. The collision set off the French ship's cargo, resulting in an explosion that could be felt over sixty miles away. The blast killed 1,635 people.

Halifax was the home of Canada's major wartime port, where troops and supplies were loaded for the perilous journey across the Atlantic to England. In December 1917, it was packed with shipping, which included the cruiser HMS *Highflyer* and the SS *Imo*, which had "Belgian Relief" on her sides to emphasise her neutrality to U-boats and was on her way to New York to load relief supplies for Belgium.

The previous evening, the *Mont Blanc* had arrived from New York, where she was loaded with a cocktail of explosives

The wreck of the freighter SS Imo in Halifax harbour, 7 December 1917

and volatile material. The ship had her holds lined with wood held together with non-sparking copper nails. However, she remained a hazard as too many volatile cargoes had been mixed together. When she entered Halifax, she was carrying 2,300 tons of wet and dry picric acid, used for making lyddite for artillery shells; 200 tons of TNT; 10 tons of gun cotton and drums of Bezol – high octane fuel – stacked on her decks. However, she arrived too late to be let through the anti submarine nets, and had to wait until the next day to enter the harbour.

On the morning of the 6 December 1917, the *Imo* weighed anchor and headed for the sea, just as the *Mont Blanc* was entering the harbour. They collided in the bottleneck known as the "Narrows". Some of the Benzol dums

broke loose and spilt on the deck. They caught fire and Captain Le Medec ordered all hands to abandon ship. Unmanned and on fire, the *Mont Blanc* drifted towards Halifax harbour where she ran into pier six in the staging area.

At around 9.05 am, the *Mont Blanc* blew up. The whole ship disintegrated in a massive explosion that killed over 1,500 people instantly including eight of the crew of HMS *Highflyer*. The blast flattened the buildings for two square miles. In all, an area of 325 acres was devastated and most of the windows in Halifax were blown out. Many spectators suffered eye injuries from the flying glass.

A mushroom-shaped cloud rose several miles into the sky, and 3,000 tons of metal rained down on Halifax. The waters of the Narrows seemed to boil

The whole ship disintegrated in a massive explosion

with shrapnel and falling rocks which had been sucked up from the harbour bed. The ship's gun landed near Alboro Lake a mile and a half away, while the stock of one of her anchors landed in a wood three miles away.

The blast caused a manmade tsunami that rocked nearby ships at their moorings and overwhelmed some smaller vessels. The wave then travelled across to the shores of Dartmouth, where it was funnelled up Tufts cove and washed away a settlement of the Micmac, the native American tribe of the area.

The blast set fire to the wooden houses. Others were set ablaze by over-turned stoves. The fire soon threatened the naval magazine at the Wellington Barracks and the area was evacuated. The magazine was then made safe by dumping its contents into the harbour. Afterwards, rescuers returned to the city but their efforts were hampered by nightfall and the onset of a blizzard.

Rumours spread that Halifax was being bombed by Zeppelins, or that it had been on the receiving end of a German Naval bombardment. Anti-German hysteria was high, survivors with German-sounding names were attacked. As it was, the port of Halifax was put out of operation and it had a devastating effect on the war effort.

Many civilians suffered burns, blindness and other injuries as a result of the explosion. The Halifax Relief Commission was established to help the injured, the bereaved and those made homeless by the accident. This organisation is still aiding the remaining survivors of the disaster, over eighty years after the explosion.

Funds poured in from around the world, even as far away as New Zealand. However, most of the relief came from the state of Massachusetts which sent not only doctors, nurses, medical supplies, food and clothing, but also transport, glass and glaziers. Every year Halifax presents Boston with a giant Christmas tree to show its gratitude.

Rumours spread that Halifax was being bombed by Zeppelins

Mary Rose 1545

On the evening of 19 July 1545, Henry VIII watched from the shore as his flagship the *Mary Rose* led the English fleet out of Portsmouth harbour to engage the French. She quickly outran the rest of the fleet and, when she came under fire, she put about to fire a broadside and to wait for support. But a sudden gust of wind caught her as she turned, causing her to heel over.

Her newly installed deck guns were seen to break loose, crashing into her leeward side and unbalancing the ship. Her lower gun-ports had not been closed. They sank beneath the water level and she quickly filled and sank.

On board were 185 soldiers, 200 seamen and thirty gunners. Most of her crew were drowned when they were trapped in the netting rigged to stop the enemy boarding. Only a handful who were working aloft survived.

At the time of her loss the *Mary Rose* was already obsolescent. Built in 1510, she had already been modified several times to carry different armaments. But by 1545, she was too cumbersome and slow to meet the challenge of galleys. The mixed battery of medium and short-range weapons was hard to combine effectively, and this type of ship became too small to carry its complement of sailors and soldiers. Henry had already developed a new type of ship, armed with heavy guns and better sailers. It was a development of his new ships that his daughter Elizabeth I used to defeat the Spanish Armada.

Early attempts to raise the *Mary Rose* failed, although some of her guns were raised at the time. Others were recovered in the 1830s, but the site was then lost and serious work on the site only began over a century later, in the 1970s. After a major archaeological investigation of the area, the *Mary Rose* was lifted in two halves in 1982. She is conserved in Portsmouth, along with over 22,000 artefacts found on board.

Like the *Titanic* before it, the *Andrea Doria* was thought to be unsinkable

The *Andrea Doria* immediately began listing badly and soon sank, taking 51 people with her

Andrea Doria
1956

At 11 pm on 26 July 1956 the Swedish cruise ship *Stockholm* sliced through the fog off Nantucket and into the side of the Italian passenger ship *Andrea Doria*. After struggling to stay afloat for twelve hours, the crippled Italian liner sank in the worst liner collision in history.

Despite the fate of the *Titanic*, the *Andrea Doria* was thought to be unsinkable. Built with the most modern technology available, she had all the newest safety equipment. In just three

Captain Piero Calamani did not make announcements, for fear of panicking the passengers

years, she had crossed the Atlantic a hundred times and was scheduled to arrive in New York Harbour the following morning.

Although both ships were equipped with radar, officers made miscalculations in thick fog and the two ships were travelling as full speed when they collided. The icebreaking bow of the Swedish ship struck the Italian liner broadside.

One of the survivors recalled seeing a large shower of sparks and hearing the crash of metal as the *Stockholm* slammed into the starboard side of the *Andrea Doria*. She immediately began to list. As the *Stockholm* reversed her engines to pull her bow out of the Italian liner's

on the *Titanic*, Captain Piero Calamani did not make announcements, for fear of panicking the passengers

An SOS brought a flotilla of rescuers led by the French liner *Ile de France* which was over two hours away. Eventually the starboard lifeboats were lowered and ropes were rigged to lower passengers into them. When she arrived the *Ile de France* picked up 753 survivors in lifeboats. Others rowed over to the *Stockholm* and were picked up. But in the chaos of the rescue, a pregnant woman jumped into the water to save her children. In all 51 people died, while 1,600 were rescued.

The badly damaged *Stockholm* was towed into New York Harbour two days later. The *Andrea Doria* was left where she lies 225 feet down.

Ironically, the fatal addition was those extra lifeboats

side, she bumped along the side of the *Andrea Doria*, making several more holes.

The *Andrea Doria* was already unstable as her huge fuel tanks were nearly empty, making her top heavy. One of her fuel tanks was holed and, as water poured in one side, the remaining fuel poured out of the other, increasing the list. It soon became clear that the Italian ship was doomed.

The list was soon so bad that most of the lifeboats were useless. Those along the port side lay against the side of the ship and could not be lowered, while those on the starboard swinging out too far for passengers to step into them. As

Eastland 1915

At 7.28 am on 24 July 1915, the excursion steamer *Eastland* slowly rolled over while she was still moored to her dock between LaSalle and Clark Streets on the south bank of the Chicago River. There were 2,572 passengers on board, largely Western Electric employees, their friends and family going to an annual company picnic in Michigan City, Indiana. In the accident, 844 perished – making the tragedy Chicago's single most deadly disaster.

The causes of the disaster are still subject to debate, but several facts are clear. The steamer had a reputation for being top-heavy and had at several times in the past been reported as listing in an alarming way. Her water–ballasting system was regarded as dangerously unstable by many persons. A series of modifications had steadily increased the top-heavy tendency of the vessel. Fearful of just such a disaster that eventually overtook the *Eastland*, more lifeboats had been added, increasing her instability.

The *Titanic* sets off on her maiden voyage from Southampton

The *Titanic* had nine decks accommodating 3,457 people

All these changes made her so unsteady that with a full passenger load of 2,500 persons she could be kept upright only through exceptional seamanship. The owners, captain and engineers were apparently not aware of the dangers posed by her instability and did not compensate properly. Thus she turned turtle the first time a full passenger load was taken aboard after her last modification. Ironically, the fatal addition was those extra lifeboats.

Lawsuits continued for more than twenty years. The *Eastland* herself was refloated, renamed the *Wilimette* and became a naval training vessel until she was broken up for scrap in 1947.

Titanic 1912

At the beginning of the 20th century, before air travel took over, huge numbers of people travelled between Europe and North America by ship. Huge liners plied the North Atlantic and the shipping companies were in competition to make the fastest crossing and provide passengers with the most luxurious surroundings.

In 1899, Thomas Ismay, the founder of the White Star Line, brought the *Oceanic* into service. This had luxury cabins with private bathrooms equipped with fresh-water taps and electric bells to summon the stewards. Ismay died in 1900 and the White Star Line was taken over by his son Bruce Ismay, who wanted to go one better. With William James Pirrie of the Belfast shipbuilder Harland & Wolff, he set about building a new generation of luxury liners. One of these would be the *Titanic*.

When the *Titanic* set off on her maiden voyage from Southampton to New York on 10 April 1912, she was the largest and most luxurious ship afloat. Her four funnels were so big that two

Captain Edward J.Smith

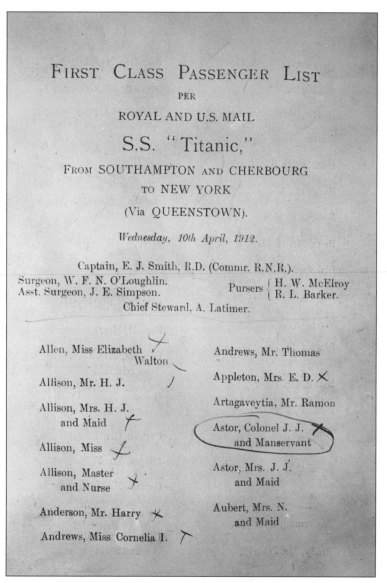

FIRST CLASS PASSENGER LIST

PER

ROYAL AND U.S. MAIL

S.S. "Titanic,"

FROM SOUTHAMPTON AND CHERBOURG

TO NEW YORK

(Via QUEENSTOWN).

Wednesday, 10th April, 1912.

Captain, E. J. Smith, R.D. (Commr. R.N.R.).

Surgeon, W. F. N. O'Loughlin.
Asst. Surgeon, J. E. Simpson.

Pursers { H. W. McElroy
{ R. L. Barker.

Chief Steward, A. Latimer.

Allen, Miss Elizabeth
Walton

Allison, Mr. H. J.

Allison, Mrs. H. J.
and Maid

Allison, Miss

Allison, Master
and Nurse

Anderson, Mr. Harry

Andrews, Miss Cornelia I.

Andrews, Mr. Thomas

Appleton, Mrs. E. D.

Artagaveytia, Mr. Ramon

Astor, Colonel J. J.
and Manservant

Astor, Mrs. J. J.
and Maid

Aubert, Mrs. N.
and Maid

The opening page of the first class passenger list. First class passengers paid over $4,000 for the best suites

trains could be driven through each of them and her propellers were the size of windmills.

Within her nine decks there would be accommodation for 3,457 people – 905 in first class, 564 in second class and 1,134 in third class. The other 944 on board were crew. The best suites cost $4,350 one way – over $80,000 in today's money. Panelled in oak, they even boasted cigar holders in the bathroom. The *Titanic* was one of the first ships to have a swimming pool. The gymnasium had the latest exercise machines from Germany. The grand staircase was lit by a chandelier and a darkroom developed passengers photographs during the voyage.

The *Titanic* was thought to be unsinkable. She had a double hull made of iron. The outer skin was an inch thick. It was divided into sixteen water-tight compartments. Four of these could be flooded without endangering the ship's buoyancy.

There were 2,224 people on board for the maiden voyage. These included John Jacob Astor – reputedly the richest man

in the world – with his young wife, and Mr and Mrs Straus, the owners of Macy's, then the world's largest department store. The owner Bruce Ismay was also on board and the ship was commanded by Captain Edward J. Smith. This was planned to be his last voyage. He was retiring after being with the White Star Line for thirty-eight years.

The *Titanic* was taking a northerly route in the hopes of making a faster passage. But it was April and the ship had received warnings that there were icebergs in the area.

At 11.40 pm the lookout Fred Fleet in the crow's nest saw one. He sounded the alarm and the engines were thrown into

On board was John Jacob Astor – reputedly the richest man in the world.

There were boats for just 1,178 of the 2,224 people on board

Some of the lucky 705 people rescued

... the great ship disappeared under the water.

reverse. But it was too late. The iceberg struck the *Titanic* a glancing blow on the starboard bow. The deck was covered with ice. Below the waterline, the iceberg had caused a huge gash. The water-tight compartments began to fill. It was then a fault in the design became apparent. The walls of the water-tight compartments did not go all the way to the deck above and, as one filled, the water spilt over into the next. Twenty minutes after the collision, five compartments were filled and it was clear that that *Titanic* was going down.

At 12.30 am Captain Smith gave the order to man the lifeboats. However, there were only sixteen wooden lifeboats and four collapsible life rafts – provision for just 1,178 out of 2,224 people on board. Women and children were to go first. By 2 am all the lifeboats had left. In the confusion, not all of them had been properly filled and 1,500 people remained on board. Some leapt into the icy waters, while others huddled together on the stern. At 2.17 am water flooded the forward compartments, raising the

stern out of the water. The hull snapped between the third and fourth funnel and the great ship disappeared under the water.

The liner *Californian* was less than twenty miles away. But its wireless operator was not on duty that night. However, the *Carpathia* had heard the *Titanic*'s distressed calls and raced to the rescue, arriving one hour and twenty minutes after she had gone down. 705 people were rescued. 1,519 lost their lives.

Following the disaster the first International Convention for Safety of Life at Sea was called in London. Under its rules, all ships had to carry enough lifeboats for all those on board. Ships had to maintain a twenty-four-hour radio watch and an International Ice Patrol was set up to warn of icebergs in the North Atlantic shipping lanes.

In September 1985, after many years of searching, the wreck of the *Titanic* was finally found in two parts by Robert Ballard. She lies in 13,100 feet of water, 400 miles off the Newfoundland coast.

THE BRIEF CAREER OF THE LARGEST LINER
DESCRIBED IN THREE TABLEAUX

DEPARTURE —THE LEVIATHAN (AND HER COMMANDER, CAPTAIN SMITH) LEAVING SOUTHAMPTON— APRIL 10

DOOM —THE FATE OF THE TITANIC, ILLUSTRATED BY ICEBERGS FLOATING IN THE ATLANTIC— APRIL 14, 10.25 P.M.

DAILY GRAPHIC
ACCIDENT £1,000 INSURANCE
TUESDAY, APRIL 16, 1912.
TITANIC SUNK: APPALLING LOSS of LIFE

DISTRESS —SCENES AT THE WHITE STAR OFFICES IN COCKSPUR STREET AND THE CITY— APRIL 15

The Titanic's first and last voyage was ill-fated from the very first, for as she was leaving Southampton the displacement of so much water caused the New York to break away from the quayside, and a collision nearly resulted. Her commander, Captain E. J. Smith, R.N., who is reported to have gone down with the liner, was captain of the Olympic when, last September, she collided with the cruiser Hawke off the Isle of Wight. Two of our pictures show a battleship in peril amid icebergs, which are submerged to the extent of seven-eighths of their bulk.

How a contemporary newspaper unfolded the events of the disaster

Empress of Ireland 1914

At around 2 am on 28 May 1914, Captain Henry Kendall of the 14,191-ton *Empress of Ireland*, bound from Quebec City to Liverpool, spotted the mast lights of the Norwegian collier *Storstad* approaching some six miles distant. But then the fog rolled in, obscuring her. If Kendall had continued on his course the two ships would have passed each other. But Kendall was a cautious man. He ordered all engines to be thrown into reverse, slowing the ship. He sounded the ship's horn three times warning other traffic of his presence and the *Empress of Ireland* and the *Storstad* exchanged warning signals in the fog.

Then suddenly Captain Kendall saw the lights of the *Storstad* reappear. They were less than ten yards away. Using a megaphone, he shouted to the commander of the *Storstad* to throw his vessel into reverse while he turned to port to minimise the impact.

The *Storstad* was still travelling at around ten knots when it struck the *Empress of Ireland* on her starboad side between her two chimneys. Water

... the engines chose this moment to break down.

The *Empress of Ireland* was struck and sunk by the Norwegian collier *Storstad*

The *Empress of Ireland* sank just 14 minutes after the initial collision

poured in so fast that people sleeping in the starboard cabins stood no chance.

Listing heavily, Captain Kendal ordered full speed ahead and turned for the shore in an attempt to run the *Empress* aground. But the engines chose this moment to break down. Suddenly all the lights went out. Five or six boats were launched successfully and those who could find their way to the side in the darkness threw themselves into the freezing water.

Just fourteen minutes after the collision, the *Empress of Ireland* sank. By that time the last frozen survivor had been fished from the water. Of the 1,477 on board, 1,012 lost their lives, including 840 passengers – eight more passengers had died than in the *Titanic* disaster.

Doña Paz 1987

In the early hours of 21 December 1987, the ferry *Doña Paz* bound from Tacloban on the island of Leyte in the Philippines to the capital Manila on Luzon, collided with the tanker Vector. Both ships sank within minutes. The *Doña Paz* was only supposed to carry 1,550 people. But in the run-up to Christmas many more were on board. In all 4,341 perished, making the sinking of the *Doña Paz* the worst ferry disaster in history.

A passing ship rescued 189 people, when the vessel sank near Bantayan Island, about three hundred miles southeast of Manila. A local journalist said that the ship had earlier been prevented from sailing out of Cebu City by port officials because it was overloaded by 81 people but was later released after a recount. Three navy ships were sent along with air force rescue helicopters. But she had sunk around 5 am and the darkness hampered the rescue.

Ships and ferries are regularly used for transport in the Philippines, an archipelago of over 7,000 islands. But the vessels are often overcrowded and accidents are frequent.

Estonia 1994

When it was acquired in 1993, the MV *Estonia* was the pride of the Estonian fleet. Built at the Meyer shipyards in Germany, the Estonia displaced 15,000 tons and was designed to withstand the often stormy conditions of the northern seas. The ship was also a symbol of the newly-independent nation of Estonia, and as such, the news of her sinking on 28 September 1994 was the more devastating.

The *Estonia* left port at Tallinn, bound for Stockholm, at around 7 pm on 28 September. Almost immediately, the weather began to deteriorate, and shortly after midnight, conditions were rough enough to force the ship's dance band to abandon playing.

Shortly before 1 am, a loud bang, which seemed to emanate from the bow-door area, was heard by some passengers and and at least one crew member. Although little notice was taken at the time, this seems to have been the moment whan the locks on the visor – the outer bow door – failed. At around 1.15 am, the visor sheared off completely. As it did so, the subsequent investigation concluded, it snagged the inner ramp, ripping it open as it did so, leaving the hull open to the waves.

As tons of water cascade in through the open hull, the *Estonia* begins to list heavily to starboard. Although no alarm

...passengers tried to traverse floors that all of a sudden loomed like cliffs above them.

is raised, passengers are already struggling to get on deck via the stairways, which are now beginning to list at a crazy angle. At 1.22 am the first SOS is sent from the *Estonia*. The message ends '…we have a problem here now, a bad list to starboard…really bad, it looks really bad here now'.

By 1.30 am the ship is heeled over at virtually ninety degrees, and passengers still trapped inside the ship are desperately trying to traverse floors that all of a sudden are looming up above them like cliffs.

Outside the ship, while some passengers and crew struggle to find life jackets and launch life-rafts, others cling to the hull, staking their lives on the belief that a ship as large as the *Estonia* will not sink beneath them. Tragically, they are wrong. At approximately 1.50 am – barely thirty minutes after the bow door was dislodged – the *Estonia*'s bow reads upwards into the sky, and she slips beneath the waves of the Baltic, and the screams from passengers still trapped inside the stricken ferry are abruptly silenced. Survivor Risto Ojassaar later remembers seeing scores of people still clinging to the ship's railings as she goes down.

Although a passenger ferry arrives on the scene at 2.12, weather conditions are appalling, and her crew struggle to pull people from the water amidst the chaos of wind and water.

Those in the water are dead by the time the first helicopters arrive, at around 3 am.

As the survivors huddle together in the life-rafts to keep out the bitter cold, the helicopters attempt to winch rafts up to safety, only to find their cables snap, plunging the would-be rescuees to their deaths. Finally, at around 9 am the last survivors are winched to safety.

The official report of the Joint Accident Investigation Commission of Estonia, Finland and Sweden concluded that the *Estonia*'s builders were at fault, although significantly it does not exonerate the crew and officers of negligence.

Sultana 1865

At 2 am on 27 April 1865, the huge side paddle steamer *Sultana* sank on the Mississippi. Some 1,547 died – exceeding even the 1,519 death toll lost on the *Titanic*. However, few people have ever heard of the sinking of the *Sultana* because news of the accident was overshadowed by one of the great events of history.

The *Sultana* had been launched two years before the American Civil War as part of the Union's strategy to carry troops and supplies up and down the Ohio, Missouri and Mississippi Rivers. After the war ended, she was sailed to Vicksburg, Mississippi, to carry the Union soldiers who had been held prisoner at the Confederate prison camp at Andersonville back north to Cairo, Illinois.

Although she was only two years old, the river boat was in decrepit condition due to her war service. But the army

The *Sultana* was loaded with 2,200 people, as well as 60 horses and 100 pigs

decided to postpone the scheduled overhaul until after the prisoners of war were returned. Most of the men were already walking skeletons. Many had to be carried on stretchers. And they were eager to get home.

The *Sultana*'s capacity was just 376, but on that fateful trip she carried 2,200 people, along with sixty horses and mules, and a hundred hogs.

On 27 April 1865, she had just passed Memphis and was fighting the strong current of the Mississippi when she was rocked by a huge explosion, followed quickly by two more. One of the *Sultana*'s boilers had blown up. A column of fire and steam shot up almost cutting the boat in two and flames engulfed the vessel. Few of those who had survived the original explosions were strong enough to swim and those who did not die in the conflagration on board, drowned.

The *Sultana* was skippered by maverick captain J Cass Mason who had just won the distinction of making the fastest trip between New Orleans and St Louis. He had arrived in Vicksburg a few weeks before on his way to New Orleans and had met the chief quartermaster. of the Mississippi, Colonel Ruben Heath who told him that the Federal Government were offering to pay $5 per enlisted man and $10 per officer to any steamboat operator who would take them back to the north. Heath was a scoundrel who had been cheating the government throughout the war and had only managed to avoid court martial through his family connections in Washington. Mason left for New Orleans while Heath arranged to collect together as many men as he could for him to pick up on the return trip.

Heath approached the officer in charge of the prisoner repatriation Captain Frederick Speed using bribes and deception. Speed in turn contacted Captains Williams and Kerns who were under pressure to empty their transit camps. When the Sultana returned to Vicksburg, over 1,400 men were ready to

board and more were arriving by train.

The *Sultana* was delayed slightly when it developed a bulge and leak in one of its four boilers. Engineers advised the captain have two boilers plates removed and replaced, but Cass refused and made do with riveting a metal patch over the defect. Boarding began on the morning of 24 April. Some of the men on board expressed their worries that she was being overloaded when they saw crew wedging large beams under the decks that were beginning to sag under the weight of passengers. They were also puzzled that so many were boarding the *Sultana* when there were other craft available.

As the boat cast off from Vicksburg docks, the *Sultana* was carrying nearly 2,100 former prisoners of war, escorted by twenty-two men of the 58th Ohio Regiment. Added to this there were ninety or so paying passengers and a crew of eight-eight – all on board a boat licensed to carry less than four hundred people. The *Sultana*'s cargo holds also carried two thousand hogsheads of sugar, each weighing 1,200 lbs, and a large alligator in a crate which Mason had bought in New Orleans as a mascot.

The first signs of trouble arose when the boat passed other vessels or sights of interest on the shore. As men moved from side to side she listed badly. This meant that the water in her boilers flowed from one side to the other, emptying one and flooding another. Then as the boat righted, steam pressure built up in the boiler that was refilling. The crew and men of the 58th Ohio tried to stop the men moving about, but the listing worsened when the sugar was unloaded at Memphis and the boat became even more top heavy.

A few men had slipped ashore and disappeared after helping to unload the sugar, but overcrowding was still a problem as the *Sultana* slipped her moorings at around midnight on the 26th. Seven miles upstream she hit a full flood current and started listing badly. The patched starboard boiler could no

The escaping steam caused horrific injuries.

Huge paddle steamers were a common sight on the Mississippi

One man spent the entire journey sitting in the steamer's dinghy.

longer take the pressure and blew. Two boilers amidships followed suit. The blast tore out the centre of the vessel ripping apart the upper decks. The area immediately above the boiler room where sick and wounded soldiers had been placed was completely destroyed.

The escaping steam caused horrific injuries. As it blasted aft, it scalded everyone in its path or flung them out into the river. More carnage resulted when one of the huge smoke stacks came crashing down. The damaged furnaces then set fire to the ship, which was fanned by the breeze blowing down the river.

At first the men in the bow area thought they were safe as the fire spread aft. But as the wreck turned in the current so the fire spread towards them. They flung anything that would float overboard and jumped in after, while others lowered themselves into the water with ropes. However months of poor food and deprivation in Confederate prisons meant that many were too weak to swim. They drowned in the river. One quick-thinking soldier saved himself making a makeshift life raft. Private

William Lugenbeal bayoneted Captain Mason's alligator and clambered aboard its crate, which carried him downstream.

An hour after the blast, the south-bound steamer *Boston II* came upon the burning *Sultana* and pulled some 150 survivors from the water. The captain of the *Boston II* then sped downstream to Memphis to raise the alarm. But the town already knew of the accident. Private Wesley Lee had been blown off the deck and had been carried downstream to Memphis where he was spotted by night-watchmen on the levee. Numerous small craft took to the water to search for survivors. However soldiers on guard at the nearby Fort Pickering had been told to be on the watch for guerrilla activity and opened fire. Fortunately, nobody was injured however and, once the situation was made clear, the soldiers joined the rescue.

Some forty or so men saved themselves by lowering themselves into the water and hanging onto the hull. When most of the *Sultana*'s superstructure had burnt away, they boarded her again. The wreck drifted into a flooded grove of trees where, shortly after the men were taken off, she sank. In all 786 people were rescued, most of whom were injured in some way. Some two hundred of these would die later in hospital. Captain Mason was among the dead, killed when the pilothouse and the officers' quarter were destroyed by the initial blast.

The survivors continued their journey on another steamer. Understandably many were reluctant to make the trip. One man spent the entire journey sitting in the steamer's dinghy.

The sinking of the *Sultana* was the worst marine disaster in American history. However, the day before, John Wilkes Booth, the man who assassinated Abraham Lincoln, had been cornered and killed. The hunt for the other conspirators was still on, so the story of the *Sultana* disaster was relegated to a few paragraphs on the back pages of the nation's newspapers and soon forgotten.

However, the authorities in Washington set up an inquiry. In all, three official investigations were held. At first it was suspected that a Confederate bomb had been smuggled on board in the coal, but this theory was quickly dismissed by engineers. Clearly other factors were to blame. Maritime experts singled out the poorly designed boilers that had been badly repaired, the top-heavy state of the craft and the lack of ballast.

Four men were found to be culpable for the overcrowding: Colonel Heath and Captains Speed, Williams and Kerns. Williams and Kerns, although being in charge of the prisoners' transportation, managed to escape censure. Heath had quit the army soon after the disaster and was beyond the jurisdiction of the military court. So Speed became the scapegoat. He was court-martialled. His defence tried to subpoena the unscrupulous Heath, but he refused to testify and as he was no longer a soldier he could not be forced to do so. Speed was found guilty on all counts and faced a dishonourable discharge. However the Judge Advocate General of the Army reviewed the case and the findings were

reversed. No one else faced any charges.

There is no memorial to the soldiers who died. Survivors sought to have one erected, but their efforts came to nothing as the public wanted to put the war behind them. Their only memorial is literary. Major Will McTeer, the adjutant of the 3rd Tennessee Cavalry which lost 213 men in the catastrophe, wrote: "There in the bosom of the Mississippi they found their resting place. No stone or tablet marked with their names or even unknown for them… flowers are strewn over the graves in the cemeteries of our dead but there are none for the men who went down with the *Sultana*. But let us remember them."

> ## "Women and children first."

Birkenhead 1852

On the evening of 25 February 1852, the British troopship *Birkenhead*, a 1,900-ton iron paddle steamer, left Simon's Town, South Africa, on the last leg of her voyage from Ireland to the Eastern Cape. On board were 600 souls. Over 200 were soldiers of the 74th Regiment of Foot. The rest were paying passengers.

On the way, she had to pass the rocks and shoals of Danger Point. The captain Robert Salmond had plotted a course that missed the point by three miles. But either because of strong currents or a compass error, the *Birkenhead* drove directly onto the rocks. Captain Salmond was below when the hull was ripped open.

There were only eight lifeboats – enough to carry 200 of the 600 aboard. Three got away carrying the women and children, while Salmond ordered the engines full astern to drag the ship off the rocks. In doing so, he made the damage worst. Below several stokers drowned and it became plain that the *Birkenhead* was going down. Colonel Alexander Seton, a thirty-seven year old Scot commanding the 74th Foot, drew

The Birkenhead drill: British soldiers go down with the ship

his men up on deck as the rigging crashed around them. He gave those who could swim permission to jump over the side and attempt to save their own lives. But as they rushed for the rails, he stopped them.

"Stand fast," he said. "I beg you, do not rush the boats carrying the women and children. You will swamp them."

Only three men disobeyed his orders and dived overboard. The rest held their ranks until, minutes later, the *Birkenhead* broke her back and disappeared under the waves. The order has ever since been issued: "Women and children first".

Kursk 2000

On 12 August 2000, the Russian nuclear submarine *Kursk* with 118 crewmen on board sank in the Barents Sea some hundred miles north-west of Murmansk. The submarine was located about 5 am the following morning. Rescue vessels arrived in the area soon after. Two attempts were made to save the trapped submariners, but the rescue craft were unable to dock with the submarine.

The *Kursk* crewmen were still alive until 14 August and signalling that there was water inside – though it was thought that most of the crew were killed immediately by an explosion or the original inrush of water. But it was not until the 16th that the Russians requested British and US help to rescue any survivors, by which time, all the crewmen were dead

Further attempts to dock with the submarine failed. But on 21 August, Norwegian divers managed to open the external hatch of the submarine, but found no sign of life.

In October the following year, the *Kursk* was lifted from the sea floor. By the end of March 2002, the bodies of 115 of the crewmen had been found and identified. A government investigation concluded that a training torpedo had gone off, detonating other torpedoes stockpiled in the forward compartment of the submarine. Men towards the aft had survived for some time in air pockets but the Russian authorities reluctance to call for help sealed their fate.

One Friday 3 November 2000, the funeral of the first victim of the disaster to be buried, Lieutenant-Captain Dmitri Kolesnikov, was held. A passage from the note he wrote while he waited to die in the hours after the accident was displayed in a frame by the closed coffin. The family has still not been given either the original or a photocopy of the note, but Kolesnikov's father had been shown it and made a transcription. It read: "15.45. It's too dark to write here, I'm trying to write blindly. It seems we have no chance – no more than ten to twenty per cent. I hope at least that someone will read this. Here is a list of the crew who are in the ninth compartment and will try to get out... Hello to everyone, there is no need to despair."

Speaking at the funeral Northern Fleet commander, Vyacheslav Popov, praised Kolesnikov for his bravery, saying: "His fate will become an example of serving the fatherland for everyone."

A postmortem examination established that Kolesnikov had died from carbon monoxide poisoning.

"15.45. It's too dark to write here, I'm trying to write blindly."

Joola 2002

On 29 August 2002 the ferry *Joola* sank off Dakar in Senegal, killing most of those on board. All the passengers raced to one side of the overcrowded ferry to take cover during a storm, causing it to capsize. The authorities said 970 of the 1,034 people on board died, but the death toll was probably much higher as children under five did not have tickets. Only sixty-four of the passengers survived.

The *Joola* was built to carry a maximum of 600 people. On 29 August, at least 500 were crowded onto the top deck alone for the sixteen-hour journey from Ziguinchor to Dakar, the capital. Some men were carrying their life's possessions on their backs, while women were laden with mangoes and palm oil which they aimed to sell in Dakar. And, as it was the low season for tourists, there were few cars in the ferry's hold to help stabilise it.

When the ferry rode into a storm, the people on the top deck were hit with wind and rain coming from starboard. To get under cover, they moved en mass to port. That movement caused a fatal shift in the ferry's centre of gravity and the ship turned turtle. At the time it was eleven hours sailing time from shore when, as a coastal ferry, it was only allowed to sail six hours from shore.

Senegal's president, Abdoulaye Wade, declared three days of national mourning and an official said: "Senegal is only a small country. More than a thousand people died, and everyone knows someone who knows someone. We are all affected by something like this."

President Wade has acknowledged his government's "obvious" responsibility for the disaster and he accepted the resignations of his transport minister, Youssouph Sakho and armed forces minister, Youba Sambou, in connection with the sinking of the Joola.

Community Disasters

London Smog
1952

For centuries, London was known for its thick "pea-souper" fogs. In fact, the acrid cloud that enveloped Britain's capital was not fog at all, but smog caused by the burning of wood and coal to keep houses warm and industry turning. This produced a lethal concoction of pollutants that lay over the city in a thick yellow blanket, the colour of pea-soup.

On Thursday 4 December 1952, warm air from the Atlantic trapped the smog in a cold, moist layer below it in what is known as a "temperature inversion". As visibility dropped trains collided. Buses ceased to run and aeroplanes were grounded. As the weekend drew on, Londoners retreated to their houses where they warmed themselves beside their coal fires – adding to the problem.

What appeared harmless fog soon became a killer

In much of London visibility dropped to less than a foot

In some places visibility dropped to less than a foot. In the docks along the banks of the Thames, people complained that they could not see their own feet and everything was covered with a thick layer of grime.

In hospitals, admissions soared. Bronchial and cardiac patients began to die. Coroners estimated the death toll from the four-day smog to be over 4,000, with another 8,000 deaths attributed to the long-term effects.

Cattle brought to London for the annual Smithfield show also suffered. Sixty of them were treated by vets. Some were saved by improvised masks made from sacking soaked with Scotch. But one died. Another twelve had to be slaughtered – but only two of the carcasses of these prime animals were deemed edible.

As a result of the disaster the Clean Air Act was passed, essentially banning coal burning in the city. This was speeded through parliament by another smog in 1956 which claimed a further thousand lives. Since then smogs – and even ordinary fogs – have been virtually unknown in London.

Bronchial and cardiac patients began to die.

Windscale, UK 1957

On 8 October 1957 technicians at the British nuclear power plant at Windscale in Cumberland, now Cumbria, northwest England were warming up a gas-cooled reactor. Inadequate temperature-measuring instrumentation meant the control room staff mistakenly thought the reactor was cooling down and needed extra heating.

At 11.05 am the control rods were withdrawn for a routine start to the

Windscale was seen as the future of energy provision

reactor's chain reaction. But the temperature was too high and a canister of lithium and magnesium (in the reactor to create tritium for a British H-bomb) burst and ignited. Burning uranium and graphite sent temperatures soaring to 2,300°F and blue flames shot out of the back face of the reactor. These early plutonium piles were cooled by massive fans blowing air through them, so the heat and contamination was carried up Sellafield's then famous concrete chimneys.

The first attempts to control the fire were disastrous. Fans were switched on, but instead of cooling the uranium fuel rods, they fanned the fire. Next carbon dioxide was pumped in to cool the flames. This was also counter-productive as, at those temperatures, the gas breaks down to produce oxygen which further fuelled the fire. The temperature in the piles soared. Engineers debated whether they could risk flooding the reactor with water. There was a danger that this could lead to a hydrogen explosion, or even an atomic explosion.

In the end they had no choice. The temperature was climbing by 20°F a minute when scientists flooded the reactor with water. The fire was extinguished after sixteen hours, leaving ten tons of radioactive fuel melted in the core. Large quantities of radioactive iodine escaped into the atmosphere along with plutonium, caesium and polonium.

At the time the government said that the wind was blowing the radioactive cloud from the fire out to sea. But in fact there was a temperature inversion, which meant that much of the radioactivity was blown inland. More radioactive fall out landed across the sea in Ireland. The UK government banned the sale of milk produced in an area of two hundred square miles around the reactor for several weeks and around two million litres of milk were poured away. It is estimated that at least 33 people have died prematurely from cancer caused by the accident.

While the famous chimneys have now been removed, the crippled remains of Britain's first nuclear reactor are still there. The core still contains molten uranium and still gives off a gentle heat. Hoses are left permanently attached as a safety precaution.

> **this could lead to … an atomic explosion.**

Aberfan, Wales 1966

Aberfan was an unspoiled valley in South Wales until 1869, when the first shaft of a coal mine was sunk there. Merthyr Vale Colliery was established and a small village of terraced houses sprang up around the pit head.

As the colliery developed a large heap of spoil – or slag – was built up. By 1918 it had reached 85 feet. A second was started which reached 90 feet. A third reached 130 feet by 1925. A fourth had reached 147 feet by November 1944, when it began to slide down the side of the hill. A fifth tip reached 171 feet by 1956, but a sixth tip had reached only 56 feet when a farmer complained it was spilling over onto his land. So a seventh tip was started, which had reached over 100 feet by the autumn of 1966. It was known to be unstable. Built over streams and springs, the water had worked away at its footing and in 1963 it had begun to slide. However, news of the slag heap's dangerous condition was hushed up.

On the morning of 21 October 1966, it began to move again. At 9.15 am, thousands of tons of spoil began sliding down the mountain side. It engulfed two farm cottages, killing those inside. Then it swept across a canal and a railway embankment and engulfed Pantglas Junior School. It demolished a further eighteen houses, damaged another school and more houses, and crushed cars before coming to a halt.

Rescue workers rushed to the scene, but after two hours they had found no one alive. In Pantglas Junior School 109 children between the ages of seven and ten died. Another seven children died

> **"In that silence you could not hear a bird or a child."**

After two hours rescue workers had found no survivors

The community was devastated by the disaster – 144 people died in the slide

Pantglas Junior School was completely demolished in the landslide

elsewhere. Five teachers were killed, along with another twenty-three adults.

One man had a lucky escape. Hairdresser George Williams was on his way to work when he heard what sounded like a jet plane. Through the fog he saw houses crashing to the ground. He was knocked over by flying debris, but he was covered by a sheet of corrugated iron and, later, rescued. He told a parliamentary tribunal that after the tip had ground to a halt, silence fell as if a radio had been turned off.

"In that silence you could not hear a bird or a child," he said.

The ship ran aground on Seven Stones Reef off Land's End

30,000 tons of oil poured from the ship's ruptured tanks

Torrey Canyon, UK 1967

On Sunday 19 March 1967 an oil tanker named the *Torrey Canyon* grounded on the Seven Stones Reef between Lands End and the Scilly Isles. She was carrying 120,000 tons of crude oil from Kuwait.

An attempt to salvage her failed and soon 30,000 gallons of oil from the ship's ruptured tanks was floating towards the Cornish coast. Royal Navy vessels sprayed detergent on the oil in an attempt to disperse it. When the *Torrey Canyon* started to break up, the British government decided to bomb the wreck in an attempt to set fire to the remaining oil.

On Tuesday 28 March 1967 the Fleet Air Arm sent Buccaneers from Lossiemouth to drop forty-two 1,000-

The RAF set the oil alight in an effort to halt its dispersal

pound bombs on the wreck. Royal Air Force Hunter jets then dropped cans of aviation fuel to make the oil blaze. Soon both sections of the wreck were on fire. In all forty-two bombs were dropped,

The local community were integral to the clean up operation

but a quarter of them missed the target. However, exceptionally high tides had put the blaze out and it took further attacks by Sea Vixens from the Naval Air Station at Yeovilton and Buccaneers from the Naval Air Station at Brawdy as well as more RAF Hunters carrying napalm to ignite the oil.

Crowds of holidaymakers were watching the spectacle from the shoreline at Lands End. Though the bombing was declared a success, the press made much of the fact that twenty-five per cent of the bombs missed a stationary target.

The oil that had already escaped covered 270 square miles. Most of this headed for the French coast, contaminating seventy-three miles of it. The oil spillage from the wreck of the Torrey Canyon was the first major environmental disaster of its kind. It would not be the last.

> **"The oil... covered 270 square miles"**

Shimanton Dam, Henan, China 1975

At the beginning of August in 1975 a series of storms deposited over three feet of rain on Henan Province in eastern China in three days. On 5 August alone seventeen inches fell – exceeding the former record by forty per cent. A second downpour on 6 August lasted sixteen hours and a third on 7 August three hours.

The Shimantan dam on the Hong River and the Banqiao dam on the Ru River were designed handle a maximum of about twenty inches over a three day period. By 8 August their reservoirs had filled to capacity and the run-off far exceeded the rate at which water could be expelled through their sluice gates. Shortly after midnight on 9 August, the water in the Shimantan reservoir rose sixteen inches above the crest of the dam, which collapsed emptying over twenty-six billion gallons of water in five hours into the river valley below.

Half-an-hour later, the water behind the Banqiao dam crested. Below it some brave souls worked in waist-deep water in the thunderstorm trying to save the embankment. As the dam began to crumble, a woman, cried: "Chu Jiaozi" – "The river dragon cometh". The collapse of the dam unleashed a wall of water twenty feet high and eight miles wide. Behind it was another 130 billion gallons of water.

Altogether sixty-two dams in the region broke. Downstream the dykes could not hold such a deluge, and they broke spreading the flood over some 4,000 square miles of farm land throughout twenty-nine counties and municipalities. The city of Huaibin where the waters from the Hong and Ru Rivers meet was washed away. There was no time to issue warnings as the wall of water was travelling at over thirty miles an hour and it knocked out the telephone system.

"Chu Jiaozi – The river dragon cometh"

Over 85,000 people were killed in the initial deluge. Another 200,000 people are thought to have perished from the ensuing famine and disease caused by drinking contaminated water. Eleven million people in the region were severely affected.

A hydrologist named Chen Xing had warned of the danger, but political officials changed his design for the largest reservoir on the plains. He also recommended that there be twelve sluice gates in the Shimantan Dam, but this was reduced to five by critics who said Chen was being too conservative. There were other areas of project where the number of sluice gates was arbitrarily reduced significantly. When Chen Xing objected he was denounced as an enemy of Mao Tse-tung's "Great Leap Forward" and was purged as a "right-wing opportunist". In the wake of the disaster he was rehabilitated. Taken with party officials on an airborne tour of the devastated area, he urged the use of explosives to clear channels for the flood waters to drain.

A worker at the Union Carbide plant in Bhopal, scene of the 1984 chemical leak

Bhopal, India 1984

In the early hours of 3 December 1984, forty-two tons of the deadly gas methyl isocynate, used in the production of insecticides, leaked from an underground storage tank at a Union Carbide plant at Bhopal in India. It spread over an area inhabited by nearly a quarter of a million people in the following forty minutes.

Many people died in their sleep. Others awoke to find themselves suffering from vomiting, dizziness, sore throats and burning eyes. Thousands arrived at hospital frothing at the mouth and choking. Many of those who had survived had been blinded. The streets were also littered with the bodies of birds and animals that had been poisoned.

The managing director of Union Carbide in India said that the accident had been caused by a faulty valve. When the chairman of Union Carbide, Warren M. Anderson, arrived in India, he was arrested, though he was released on bail a few days later. A $15 billion class action suit was filed against the company.

Over 2,500 people were killed and 200,000 injured at the time. According to some estimates, more than 16,000 people have died since as a result of their exposure. Some 50,000 people are still suffering significant long term effects and over 500,000 have filed injury claims with the Bhopal Compensation Court.

To date, there have been no criminal verdicts issued in the Bhopal case. But in 1989, Union Carbide settled with the Indian government for $470 million. Survivors have received $3,300 for the loss of a family member and $800 for a permanent disability. Union Carbide has since abandoned its Bhopal plant.

Bodies laid out in the street for burial after the Bhopal disaster

Repair crews set to work on the Chernobyl nuclear plant, in the Ukraine

Chernobyl, USSR
1986

On 6 April 1986, the worst-ever accident in the history of nuclear power occurred at the Soviet power station ten miles north of the city of Chernobyl in the Ukraine.

The previous evening, technicians working on Reactor Four shut down the safety systems while removing the control rods from the core. At 1.23 am on 26 April, the reactor went out of control. A series of explosions blew the top off the reactor and the resulting fire released huge amounts of highly-radioactive material into the air. The following day the 30,000 residents of the nearby city of Pripyat had to be evacuated.

On 28 April, Swedish monitoring stations noted a rise in levels of radioactivity and asked for an explanation. It was only on 4 May that the Soviet authorities admitted that there had been an accident at Chernobyl and the first detailed account was published in the Soviet newspaper *Pravda* on 6 May.

Workers risked their lives to extinguish the fire with the boots of fire-fighters sinking in molten asphalt. The reactor core was encased in the steel-and-concrete sacrophagus, which has later proved to be structurally unsound and will have to be replaced. Other radioactive debris was buried. The initial accident caused the deaths of at least thirty-two people. Dozens contracted radiation sickness. Many times more radioactive fallout was pumped into the atmosphere than that by the bombs dropped on Hiroshima and Nagasaki combined. Huge areas of the Ukraine, Belarus and Russia were contaminated and the effects spread far across Europe, including Italy, France and the UK.

A second accident occurred in 1991, when Reactor Two caught fire and was shut down. The other two reactors have since been decommissioned.

There are a number of drilling platforms scattered across the North Sea

Piper Alpha, North Sea 1988

At about 10 pm on 6 July 1988 an explosion occurred in the gas compression module on the Piper Alpha oil drilling platform in the North Sea, 110 miles north east of Aberdeen. It knocked out the main control room and main power supply, and started a large fire in the oil separation module. This fire was fed by oil from the platform and a leak in the main pipe line which carried oil from other drilling platforms to the shore. A massive plume of black smoke engulfed the north end of the platform. Ten minutes later there was a second major explosion and the platform collapsed.

There were 226 men on the platform at the time. Sixty-two were on duty. The rest were in the accommodation module. After the initial explosion, emergency systems had broken down and smoke and flames made evacuation by helicopter or lifeboat impossible. Personnel on diving duty and those working on the

the worst oil spill in US history

northern end and the lower levels of the platform escaped by jumping into the sea. But at no point was there a systematic attempt to lead men out of the accommodation module. One hundred and thirty-five died.

Exxon Valdez, Alaska 1989

Just after midnight on 24 March 1989, the *Exxon Valdez*, an oil tanker, hit Bligh Reef in the Prince William Sound, Alaska, dumping eleven million gallons of crude oil into its pristine waters. This was the worst oil spill in US history.

At almost a thousand feet long, the *Exxon Valdez* was one of the largest vessels at sea at the time. After leaving the Alaska pipeline terminal, her captain Joseph Hazelwood had retired for the night, leaving the third mate Gregory Cousins in command. He had ordered the helmsman to steer to starboard into

The effects on the local environment were devastating

the southbound shipping lane, but the vessel did not turn sharply enough and hit the reef at 12.04 am.

The oil spilt out so fast that it created waves of oil three feet above the surface of the water. By the time clean-up crews arrived ten hours later, the slick covered several miles. The chemical dispersants dropped from aeroplanes depended on wave action to work and the water in the sound was too calm for them to be effective. By the third day, the oil had covered a hundred square miles. There were not enough containment booms to prevent it spreading and it was soon threatening the country's richest concentrations of wildlife. It also threatened the livelihood of the local fishing industry and native villagers, affecting about 34,000 fishermen, some 4,000 native Alaskans, and several thousand more Alaska residents.

Exxon led the clean up effort with 11,000 workers in the summer months, spending some $2 billion dollars on the operation. A further $1 billion was spent on settling related court cases. Sea otter rehabilitation centres were established and salmon and herring fisheries were isolated and monitored. Years later, scientists were still attempting to determine the ecological damage caused by the spill.

Fishing stocks have still not fully recovered from the oil spill

Thousands upon thousands make the annual Haj pilgrimage to Mecca

Pilgrims travel from around the globe on the Haj pilgrimage to Mecca

Mecca Stampede 1990

The annual Haj pilgrimage to Mecca is the most important event of the Islamic year, atracting thousands of pilgrims annually. At the climax of the pilgrimage

The Mecca Whirl – but the celebrations turned to horror on 2 July 1990

to Mecca on 2 July 1990, more than 5,000 people were crammed into a tunnel 500 yards long designed to hold a thousand. Pilgrims pushing forward caused seven to fall at the entrance. Finding their way blocked those following turned back, only to collide with other pilgrim groups. When the elec-tricity failed there was panic. With no ventilation, the temperature soared to over 104°F. Some 1,426 people were suf-focated or trampled to death.

It was "God's unavoidable will," said King Fahd of Saudi Arabia. "Had they not died there, they would have died elsewhere at the same moment."

Lake Nyos, Cameroon 1986

At 9 pm on the night of 21 August 1986, the herdsmen and farmers living around Lake Nyos in the Cameroon were finishing their evening meal or were already in bed when they heard a distant rumble. No one took any notice. It was the rainy season and thunder was common. Within moments 1,700 lay dead.

A seismic disturbance had released a huge bubble of carbon dioxide that had accumulated at the 600 foot depths of Lake Nyos. It had been collecting there for centuries. Carbon dioxide is denser than air and a mile wide gas cloud rolled over the surrounding hills into the adjacent valleys, suffocating everyone.

There were so few survivors that the news took days to get out. The disaster was only discovered when a government worker stopped his motorbike to remove a dead antelope from the road. Soon after he felt dizzy, then began seeing dead bodies scattered along his route.

In the outlying villages some had some warning of the invisible killer when people started vomiting blood. But when they fled, they found that the roads were crammed with corpses – so many that they had to step on them.

At first rescue workers had no idea what had happened. But then it was noticed that the waters of Lake Nyos had changed colour from blue to reddish brown because the escaping gas had churned up iron from the bottom.

The community around Lake Nyos is agricultural

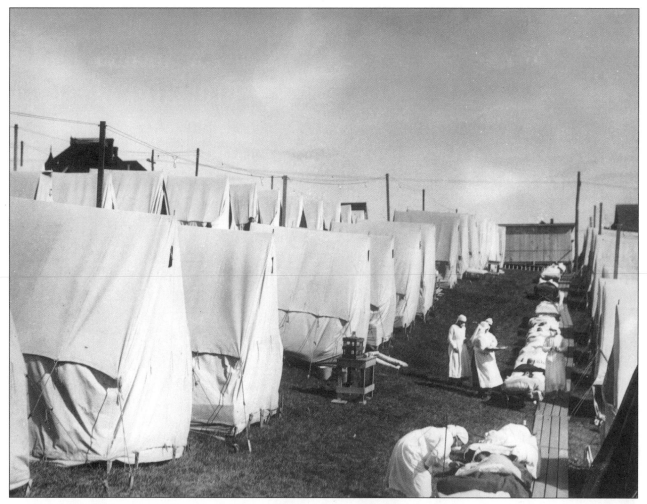

Makeshift field hospitals were set up to deal with the vast number of sufferers

World Influenza Epidemic, 1918-1919

The worldwide influenza epidemic of 1918-1919 was the worst outbreak of flu in the twentieth century and clocked up the largest death toll of any pandemic in human history.

It first appeared in early March 1918 at Camp Funston, Kansas, among US troops being trained to fight in World War I. When they went to France, they took the virus with them. The disease spread quickly and by July it had reached Poland. But this strain of the virus was comparatively mild. In August 1918, the virus seems to have mutated into a more lethal variety, killing its victims within two days. It was also more contagious. Six days after the first cases of influenza were reported at Camp Devens,

Masks were a common sight at the height of the epidemic, particularly amongst public workers

All public transport was 'fumigated' in an effort to stall the progress of the flu virus

Massachusetts, there were 6,674 on the sick list.

When World War I ended in November, troops returning home from Europe carried the virus around the world. At the height of the epidemic, New York suffered 851 deaths on a single day. Entire eskimo villages were wiped out and the casualty rate on some islands in the South Seas hit twenty per cent.

In the US, 550,000 people died – nearly ten times the number lost in the war. India is thought to have lost 12.5 million. World-wide, thirty million people are known to have perished.

Potato Famine, Ireland 1845

In 1845, the Great Potato Famine struck Ireland. It was by no means the first time the Irish crop had been blighted. Over the previous hundred years, the potato crop had failed twenty times. But this

Starving people begging for food were a common sight at the height of the famine

time, the crop failure became a catastrophe. Within four years 1.1 million Irish people would be dead, another 1.5 million had been forced to emigrate.

The potato blight had already ravaged crops in North America. But in 1845, it turned up without warning in Europe. The summer of 1845 was warm and the Irish countryside was thick with bright potato flowers. Although Irish peasant farmers planted corn as a cash crop to pay rent to their landlords, potatoes were their staple diet and everyone was delighted by the prospect of a bumper crop. No one suspected that anything was wrong until the autumn when the leaves of the potato plants began to curl at the edges and turn black. Still no one foresaw the catastrophic consequences. When the crop was lifted, the potatoes

Whole families worked tirelessly in their struggle to stave off starvation

themselves seem unaffected. However, they soon went black and turned into a squelchy, stinking mess. Vast areas of the country were affected. Within a year, men, women and children would be seen starving, naked and reduced to a state of total despair.

County Cork was particularly badly hit. Local magistrate Nicholas Cummins wrote to Sir Charles Trevelyan in the Treasury in London saying: "The alarming prospect cannot be exaggerated. In the whole city and port of Cork there is only 4000 tons of food stuff. Unless great amounts reach us from other quarters, the prospect is appalling. I assure you that unless something is immediately done the people must die..."

Relief committees were set up, but had to close after a few days as supplies ran out. Some 2,130 died in the City of Cork workhouse between December 1846 and April 1847.

Cummins wrote a letter describing the situation to the Duke of Wellington, formerly prime minister then minister without portfolio. It was published in *The Times* on Christmas Eve 1846 and described a trip to a country village.

"Being aware that I would have to witness scenes of frightful hunger, I provided myself with as much bread as five men could carry," Cummins wrote, "and on reaching the spot, I was surprised to find the wretched hamlet apparently deserted. I entered some of the hovels to ascertain the cause, and the scenes that presented themselves were such as no tongue or pen can convey the slightest idea of. In the first, six famished and ghastly skeletons, to all appearances dead, were huddled in a corner on some filthy straw, their sole covering what seemed a ragged horsecloth, their wretched legs hanging about, naked above the knees. I approached with horror, and found by low moaning that they were still alive – they were in fever, four children, a woman, and what had once been a man. It was impossible to go through the detail. Suffice it to say, that in a few minutes, I was surrounded by at least two hundred such phantoms, such frightful spectres as no words can describe, suffering either from famine or from fever. Their demoniac yells are still ringing in my ears and their horrible images fixed on my brain."

Public works were begun in an effort to bring relief, but this only meant that poor starving wretches were forced to labour in work details.

"It was melancholy and degrading in the extreme to see the women and girls

The death carts did swift business – within four years 1.1 million people had died

withdrawn from all that was decent and proper and labouring in mixed gangs on the public roads," wrote one English observer.

Some 750,000 people were employed in such a way. But this left three million supported by public funds.

The famine brought diseases to Ireland with it. The most common was oedema.

"Many of the people were prostrate under that horrid disease – the results of long continued famine and low living – in which first the limbs, and then the body, swell most frightfully, and finally burst," one eyewitness wrote. "Perhaps the poor children presented the most piteous and heart-rending spectacle. Many were too weak to stand, their little limbs attenuated, except where the frightful swellings had taken the place of previous emaciation. Every infantile expression entirely departed; and in some reason and intelligence had evidently flown."

Scurvy struck, causing people's teeth to drop out and their legs to turn black with broken blood vessels. Few could afford to wash or change their clothes or bedding. Their filthy rags were infested with lice, which brought with it typhus. Its victims vomited uncontrollably and were covered with sores and rashes. Their faces swell and turn black and their whole body gives off an unbearable stench. For fear of the disease, parents abandoned their children and children their parents. Corpses were left unburied. There were riots and, by 1848, Ireland was in open rebellion. It climaxed with a farcical shootout at Widow McCormack's house in County Tipperary where, due to a misunderstanding, one rebel was killed and several others wounded.

As a consequence of the famine, the population of Ireland dropped from 8.4 million in 1844 to 6.6 million in 1851. Even flight was no guarantee of survival. One in six of the people emigrating died on board ship.

Perhaps inevitably, the Irish blamed the disaster on the English. The government in London resented this as it had provided £8 million in relief. But much of it was badly organised. Throughout the famine grain, meat and other high-quality foodstuffs were exported from Ireland because Irish peasant farmers did not have the money to pay for it.

This resentment led to the pressure for Home Rule, and then ultimately to independence in 1921. By then Ireland's population was barely half what it had been in the 1840s.

"I was surrounded by at least two hundred such phantoms"

Volcanoes

Pompeii, Italy AD 79

On 24 August, AD 79, Gaius Plinius Secundus – better known as Pliny the Elder – was settling down for an afternoon's reading at his house at Misenum at the mouth of the Bay of Naples when his sister asked him to come and have a look at a strange cloud.

He climbed to the top of a nearby hill. An account of what he saw was transcribed by his nephew, Pliny the Younger: "The cloud was rising; watchers from our distance could not tell from which mountain, though later it was known to be Vesuvius. In appearance and shape it was like a tree – the umbrella pine would give the best idea of it. Like an immense tree trunk, it was projected into the air, and opened out with branches."

It was not known that Vesuvius was a dormant volcano. It had not erupted within living memory and its slopes were covered with orchards, vineyards and olive groves. At its foot lay the commercial and agricultural centre of Pompeii and the resort of Herculaneum – which boasted an amphitheatre that could seat 16,000, dozens of taverns, magnificent brothels and lavishly appointed baths.

However, there were some tell-tale signs. The Greek geographer Strabo had remarked that Vesuvius was shaped like a volcano. Twenty miles away at the Phegrean Fields were reputed to be the gates of Hades – complete with smoke-filled caverns and volcanic

> "Like an immense tree trunk, it was projected into the air..."

Pompeii still stands today, a haunting reminder of the volcano's power

geysers. There was also seismic activity in the area. An earthquake had destroyed Pompeii and Herculaneum sixteen years before and they had had to be rebuilt.

At around midday on 24 August 79, Vesuvius had broken open with a sound like a thunderclap and fire, ash and pumice had shot twelve miles into the sky. Pliny the Elder realised that he was witnessing a major natural event. He ordered a galley to be made ready so that the could get a closer look and asked his seventeen year old nephew to accompany him. Pliny the Younger declined on the grounds that he had to study. Meanwhile his uncle received a note from a friend asking him to come and rescue her.

Most were simply overcome where they stood.

By this time Vesuvius was pelting Pompeii with ash and pumice. Rocks as much as eight inches across were falling from thousands of feet in the air, killing anyone they hit. The build-up of pumice caused roofs to collapse and the inhabitants fled. Then a dark cloud descended over Misenum, wreathing the town in what Pliny the Younger called "the darkness of a sealed room without lights".

By evening, Pliny the Elder had reached the fishing village of Stabiae, which was being shaken by violent tremors. He kept his nerve, taking a leisurely bath before going to bed. The following morning Pliny the Elder died. He had either been suffocated by sulphurous gas, or his weak heart had given out because of the difficulty he had breathing.

Thinking the worst was over, some Pompeiians returned to their city when a pyroclastic flow – a deadly mixture of ash, pumice and super-heated steam – came surging down the mountain at sixty miles an hour. Most were simply overcome where they stood. Their bodies were then covered with between nineteen and twenty-three feet of pumice and ash, keeping them perfectly preserved until excavation of the site began in the nineteenth century.

Vesuvius looms over Pompeii, once a bustling commercial centre

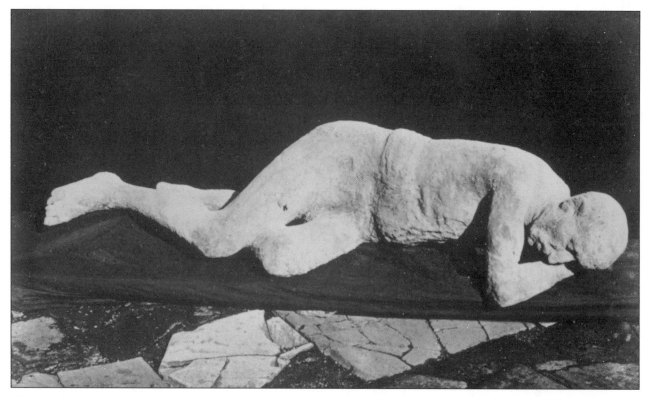

Many residents of Pompeii were covered with over 20 feet of pumice and ash, preserving them forever

Herculaneum had escaped most of the first day's horrors. While twelve feet of pumice and ash had landed on Pompeii, only eight inches had fallen on Herculeneum. But then, without warning, the residents were hit by a surge of super-heated steam that came rolling down the mountain. A boiling avalanche followed, smashing the buildings to pieces and searing everything in its path with temperatures of up to 500°C. Hundreds sought refuge in the archways of the Suburban Baths overlooking the sea. But the water offered no protection. The sea pulled back, then came crashing back towards them while the scalding avalanche was at their backs.

An hour later another scalding cloud arrived, killing any survivors. In all six surges hit the town, burying Herculeum under sixty feet of volcanic debris that turned into solid rock. While the ash and pumice that covered Pompeii could be shovelled away, the rock that covered Herculeneum had to be removed by drill and chisel when the excavation began in 1980. Beneath it, as at Pompeii, there was a perfect time capsule. The people of Herculeneum had been preserved exactly

as they were, going about their everyday business nineteen centuries before.

... the residents were hit by surge of super-heated steam...

Skaptarjökul, Iceland 1783

On 11 June 1783, the volcano Skaptarjökul on Iceland began to erupt. After a series of violent earthquakes, the sides of the mountain cracked and lava poured out. A stream of molten rock 200 feet wide and up to 600 feet deep filled a nearby river gorge and overflowed, filling a lake and an area honeycombed with caves.

There were further lava flows on 18 June and 3 August. The amount of material ejected is estimated to have the mass of Mont Blanc in France and the outflow, at its peak, rivalled that of the Amazon, the world's largest river.

The lava overwhelmed twenty villages. It is thought that more than 9,000 people were killed, out of a total Icelandic population of 50,000 at the time. Over 190,000 sheep, 28,000 horses and 11,000 head of cattle also died. This massive loss of life was caused by the streams of lava, toxic gas and floods caused by lava blocked rivers. And a subsequent famine resulted from the destruction of plant life and the disappearance of fish – the Icelandic staple – from the coastal waters.

The ejection of vast amounts of ash into the atmosphere had a cooling effect. Benjamin Franklin noted that the sunlight reaching the ground in 1783 was diffused. A strange "dry fog" hung over the land and when the rays of the sun "were collected in the focus of a burning glass, they would scarcely kindle brown paper". Franklin himself suggested that "vast quantities of smoke" emitted from Skaptarjökul was responsible for this. However, the volcano Asamayama in Japan had also erupted that year, expelling a vast amount of ash and red-hot rocks which fell on nearby villages, killing five thousand. One rock measured more than 260 feet by 120 feet and was said to have formed an island where it landed. Together, the two volcanoes seem to have been responsible for the cooling Franklin noted.

Mt Tambora, Indonesia 1815

In 1815, the 13,000-foot volcano Tambora near Java erupted, causing a disaster whose effects were felt worldwide.

Since Europeans had first set foot in Indonesia, Tambora had been thought to be extinct. But in 1814 it began to emit small showers of ash. Then on the night of 5 April 1815, there was an earthquake. This was followed by a series of explosions, some of which were heard nine hundred miles away in Sumatra. The most violent eruption occurred on the night of 11-12 April and the explosions continued until July. In all more than thirty-six cubic miles of solid material was blasted into the air, leaving the mountain a mile shorter than before. Ash and smoke darkened the sky even at midday. Rocks the size of a human head fell in the vicinity. The sky was darkened for some 300 miles and ash fell up to 800 miles away.

Subsidence left the village of Tomboro submerged under eighteen feet of water.

Every strata of Javanese society was affected by the eruption of the volcano near Tambora

Some 12,000 people died in the eruption. A further 80,000 died of starvation and disease caused by the devastation of the area.

Sir Stamford Raffles, founder of the British colony of Singapore, was serving as military governor of Java when Tambora erupted. He reported that the sky was dark at noon and falling ash covered the island. Glowing lava could be seen on top of the cone and he heard what sounded like the sound of artillery or distant thunder.

Eruption left the mountain almost a mile shorter than it was before and the collapse of the caldera caused an earthquake which was felt more than three hundred miles away. Another earthquake shook the island on 13 January 1909. Around that time lava began to flow from a cone that had begun forming in the caldera in 1847.

The effects of the 1815 eruption were felt around the world. Much of the material ejected from the volcano was in the form of fine ash, which was blasted into the atmosphere. There was so much of it that the amount of sunlight falling on the Earth was cut significantly. This caused a dramatic drop in temperature across the globe and 1816 became known as "the year without a summer". Snow fell in New England in July. Although the US was able to feed itself – its crops were adequately adapted for the colder climate – there was famine in Canada and Northern Europe, where people were reduced to eating rats. In Switzerland, grain prices rose fourfold. France was particularly hard hit because crop failures there came on the back of the devastation of the Napoleonic Wars. Farmers who dared to take their produce to market needed armed escorts to prevent them being attacked and robbed by starving mobs along the way.

Although the catastrophic summer of 1816 has not been definitively tied to the eruption of Tambora – it fell within the normal range of climatic fluctuations – similar cold spells have been seen after other major eruptions. After the

"the year without a summer"

eruption of Krakatoa in 1884 the sunlight falling on the Earth was sixteen per cent down from the previous year and twelve per cent below the norm. It dropped by four per cent after Alaska's Bogoslov and several other volcanoes erupted in 1889. A drop of thirteen per cent was recorded after the eruption of Mount Pelée and Soufrière in 1902. Some seventeen per cent of solar radiation was obscured after the eruption of Mount Katmai in Alaska in 1912. It is also likely that climate change after the eruption of the volcano on the Greek island of Santorini in ancient times put paid to the Minoan civilisation on Crete.

Cotopaxi, Ecuador 1877

The volcano Cotopaxi stands 19,812 feet tall thirty-five miles from Quito, the capital of Ecuador. It had erupted at least fifty times since 1738. In 1877 molten lava from the crater melted ice and snow on the summit. The resulting melt-water

The volcano Cotopaxi is 35 miles from Quito, Ecuador's capital

caused flooding up to 200 miles away and is thought to be responsible for the death of over a thousand people.

Like all the countries of the western seaboard of South America Ecuador is also prone to earthquakes. On 5 August 1949, an earthquake of 7.5 on the Richter scale devastated 1,500 square miles. Its centre was twenty-five miles below the surface. Over fifty towns and cities were severely damaged. Around 6,000 people were killed; another 20,000 injured and 100,000 left homeless. The total damage was estimated at $60 million.

Mt Pelée, Martinique 1902

The French colonised the Caribbean island of Martinique in 1635 and built its commercial capital, St Pierre, at the foot of a seemingly extinct volcano they called Mont Pelée. However, in 1792, it began to rumble and a few spouts of ash dusted the upper slopes. Then in 1851, it rumbled another warning, this time dusting the prosperous suburbs of St Pierre with ash. But the rain came and washed the ash away and everyone forgot about the volcano.

By the turn of the twentieth century, St Pierre was a town of 30,000 people. It had a cathedral, several parish churches, a military hospital, cafés, dancehalls and a theatre where visiting productions from Paris were performed. And on sunny days, the Martiniquais like to picnic on the slopes of Mont Pelée and bathe in the clear waters of the lake on its peak.

In April 1902, the mountain began to rumble again and a vent around the summit began to belch sulphurous gases. On 23 April there were tremors and a light rain of cinders fell on the southern and western slopes. Then on 25 April the mountain began to blast rock and ashes high into the sky.

At 11.30 pm on the night of 2 May, there was a massive explosion and the pillar of black smoke that climbed from

St Pierre was a town of 30,000 people, established at the base of Mont Pelée

Mont Pelée erupts and the destruction begins

the summit was wreathed with lighting. But in the morning Pierrotins found their city undamaged, but covered once more in a light dusting of white ash, like a fresh fall of snow. By 4 May, the cloud of ash was so dense that ships were afraid to sail through it. The sea bobbed with dead birds and a number of peasant children from outlying regions were seen wandering around the city in a daze. The following day, the electrical disturbances around the summit were so intense that they knocked out the power in the city. More peasants poured into the city from outlying regions, bringing their live-stock. Some Pierrotins began to take flight to nearby Guadeloupe.

On the morning of 7 May the pas-senger ship Roraima dropped anchor in the harbour and another steamer, the Roddam, moored close inshore so the passengers could view the volcano. It was Ascension Day and, that evening while the populace of St Pierre were at church,

the telegraph operator at the post office began sending his daily report to the capital Fort-de-France, eleven miles away. At 7.52 pm, the telegraph line went dead and Fort-de-France was plunged into darkness.

The crew of the *Pouyer-Quertier*, a repair ship eight miles off shore, saw the side of Mont Pelée open. A huge black cloud shot out horizontally while a mushroom cloud curled up into the sky. The horizontal cloud rolled noiselessly down the slope towards the city, clinging to the ground like a heavy gas. Inside it there was an incandescent glow and flashes of lighting. When the cloud enveloped the city, everything it touched burst into flames. On the quayside, a thousand barrels of rum exploded in a huge roar. Even on board the *Pouyer-Quertier* the crew could feel the heat and red-hot rocks rained down on her decks.

Further out to sea the Comte de Fitz-James, with his travelling companion

"From the depths of the earth came rumblings, an awful music which cannot be described."

The devastation in St Pierre was total

The town became a sea of rubble

Baron de Fontenilliat, also witnessed the destruction of St Pierre. He wrote: "From a boat in the roadstead, I witnessed the cataclysm that came upon the city... From the depths of the earth came rumblings, an awful music which cannot be described. I called my companion's name, and my voice echoed back at me from a score of angles. All the air was filled with the acrid vapours that had belched from the mouth of the volcano...

"We saw the shipping destroyed by a breath of fire. We saw the cable ship *Grappler* keel over in the whirlwind, and sink as through drawn down into the waters of the harbour by some force from below. The *Roraima* was overcome and burned at anchor. The *Roddam*... was able to escape like a stricken moth which crawls from the flame that has burned its wings..."

The following day the governor sent a warship to find out what had happened to St Pierre. The Comte de Fitz-James followed its landing party ashore.

"When we got ashore we called aloud, and only the echo of our voices answered us. Out fear was great, but we did not know which way to turn, and had it been our one thought to escape we would not have known how to do so. It was about one o'clock in the afternoon when we reached the shore. Our weariness was beyond description. Sleep was the one thing that I wanted, but I overcame the desire and, with Baron de Fontenilliat, set off to make our way to St Pierre, hoping that we might render some assistance to the injured..."

But they found no one and entered a strange, alien landscape.

"We saw great stones that seemed to

The grim effects of the erupting Mt Pelée

be marvels of strength, but when touched with the toe of a boot they crumbled into impalpable dust. I picked up an iron bar. It was about an inch and a half thick and three feet long. It had been manufactured square, then twisted to give it more strength. The fire that came down from Mont Pelée had taken from the iron all of its strength. When I twisted it, it fell into filaments, like so much broom straw…"

But otherwise things seemed remarkably undamaged.

"I know that the explosion of Mont Pelée was not accompanied by anything like an earthquake, for… when we entered St Pierre we found the fountains all flowing, just as though nothing had happened."

Some 30,000 people were dead. Superheated steam with temperatures of over 1000°C, mixed with lethal gas and red-hot ash to create a pyroclastic flow, and had overcome them. Their clothing had been ripped from them as if they had been hit by a cyclone. Some were burnt

The sea bobbed with dead birds...

beyond recognition; others appeared untouched. Some seem to have perished so suddenly they had no time to react; others died horribly.

Extraordinarily, there was a survivor. He was a convicted murderer named Ludger Sylbaris, who had been locked in an underground cell. He said that hot, dark air mixed with ash had come through the bars, burning his flesh. He cried out in agony, but no one came to help him. For four days, he remained locked in his cell, knowing nothing of the fate of the city. The salvage workers heard his moans and dug him out. As Mont Pelée had reprieved him, so did the authorities. He later toured with Barnum & Bailey.

St Pierre burnt for days and it took weeks to bury the dead. In October a lava dome began to form, raising the height of Mont Pelée by a thousand feet. The city never recovered. It was rebuilt, though on a much smaller scale. Mont Pelée erupted again in 1929, but this time St Pierre was evacuated.

Nevado del Ruiz, Columbia 1985

After fifty-one weeks of minor earthquakes and spouts of steam, Columbia's tallest volcano Nevado del Ruiz exploded violently at 3.06 pm on 13 November 1985. Two hours later pumice fragments and ash were showering down on the town of Armero. The mayor went on the radio and assured citizens that there was no danger. But the Red Cross ordered an evacuation of the town at 7 pm. Shortly afterwards though, the ash stopped falling. The evacuation was called off and calm was restored.

Two hours afterwards, molten rock began to erupt from the summit crater and melt the mountain's snow cap. But storm clouds obscured the summit area and no one below could see what was going on. Meltwater mixed with ash creating hot "lahars" – or volcanic mudflows. One flowed down the gorge of the

The Red Cross evacuated Armero when Nevado del Ruiz first erupted. They later played a vital part in the aftermath of the disaster.

River Cauca and submerged the village Chinchina, killing 1,927 people. Another, travelling at over thirty miles an hour, burst through a dam on the River Lagunillas and arrived at Armero at eleven pm. Most of the town was swept away or buried in only a few short minutes, killing most of the townspeople.

No one should have been surprised. A similar lahar had flowed down the River Lagunillas in 1595, killing 636 people. In 1845, another lahar had killed over a thousand people. Indeed, the original village of Armero was built directly on top of the 1845 mudflow.

Columbian geology student José Luis Restrepo was in Armero when the lahar hit in 1985.

"We didn't hear any kind of alarm," he said. "When the ash started falling, we turned on the radio. The mayor was talking and he said that we should not worry and should stay calm in our houses. Suddenly the local radio station went off the air. About fifteen seconds later, the electric power went out. That's when we started hearing noises that sounded like something toppling. We didn't hear anything else, no alarm. When we went out, the cars were swaying and running people down. There was total darkness. The only light was provided by car headlights. We were running and were about to reach the corner when a river of water came down the streets. We turned around screaming and ran back towards the hotel. The waters were dragging beds along, over-turning cars, sweeping people away. We went back to the hotel. It was a three-storey building with a terrace, built of cement and very sturdy. Suddenly, I heard bangs, and looking towards the rear of the hotel I saw something like foam, coming down out of the darkness. It was a wall of mud. It crashed into the rear of the hotel, smashing the walls. Then the ceiling slab fractured. The entire building was destroyed and smashed to pieces."

Even the sturdily built concrete structure of the hotel could not resist.

> ... the cars were swaying and running people down.

The boulder-filled wall of mud quickly razed the city like "a wall of tractors".

The university bus in the parking lot next to the hotel was lifted up on the wave of mud and exploded.

"I covered my face, thinking I was going to die horribly," said Restrepo. "There was a little girl who I thought was decapitated, but her head was buried in the mud. A lady said to me: 'Look, that girl moved a leg.' Then I moved toward her and my legs sank into the mud, which was hot but not burning, and I started to get the little girl out, but then I saw her hair was caught."

When rescuers arrived at Armero the following day, they found a tangle of trees, cars and mutilated bodies scattered throughout an ocean of grey mud. Injured survivors lay moaning in agony while rescue workers struggled frantically to save them. In all some 23,000 people and 15,000 animals were killed. Another 4,500 people were injured and some 8,000 people were rendered homeless. The estimated cost of the disaster is $1 billion, or about one-fifth of the Columbia's Gross National Product.

The tragedy could have been averted. Nevado del Ruiz had been giving warning signs in the form of minor earthquakes and steam jets for nearly a year. A scientific commission had visited the crater in late February and a report of the volcanic activity appeared in the newspaper La Patria in early March. By July, seismologists in various other countries plotted the magma rising under the volcano. A UN-funded report by the National Bureau of Geology and Mines concluded that even with a moderate eruption there was "a hundred per cent probability of mudflows... with great danger for Armero, Ambalema, and the lower part of the River Chinchina". This was published six weeks before the disaster, but only ten copies were circulated. Government officials dismissed the report as "too alarming" and refused to evacuate people. However, a group of scientists visited the crater on 12 November and reported no imminent danger.

Mt Pinatubo, Phillipines 1991

Prior to 1991, Mount Pinatubo on the Philippine island of Luzon was a relatively unknown volcano with a heavily forested lava dome and no historical record of activity. But its 1991 eruption was one of the largest of the twentieth century. At least 847 people died, many as a result of the typhoon that followed it. A million people were at risk and the death toll would have been much higher if scientists had not predicted the eruption and had the area evacuated.

Pinatubo had lain dormant for 40,000 years until 2 April 1991, when an explosion devastated about a quarter of a square mile of forested land, stripping leaves and vegetation over several square miles, and depositing ash eight miles away. There were no injuries or deaths that time, but some 2,000 people were evacuated.

Seismic activity continued from April to mid-May. On 12 June, twelve hours of tremors and minor explosions were followed by a major blast that threw ash and rocks fifteen miles into the air. Debris fell up to twelve miles away.

Infrared monitors from the nearby US Clark Air Force Base were used to monitor the volcano as it collapsed in on itself, leaving the summit 450 feet lower than before. More explosions razed all vegetation within a mile of the crater and trees five miles away were defoliated.

From 14 to 16 June explosions continued, mixing ash and volcanic debris with the heavy rain from the typhoons that had then hit. Secondary explosions were caused by rain falling into the lake of lava forming in the crater. More than 212,500 acres of farmland and fish farms were destroyed and 650,000 people were put out of work. Further eruptions continued until 1995.

Soufrière Hills, Montserrat 1995

Since British settlers arrived there in 1632, Montserrat had been considered an island paradise. But in 1995 a long-dormant volcano turned the island into a living hell.

The volcano on Montserrat had not erupted in historic times and was thought to be so harmless that it was known only as the Soufrière Hills. But on 18 July 1995, it began to erupt. As lava encroached on outlying farms, people had to be evacuated. However, the volcano was still considered to be relatively benign. But then, although the volcano was continuously monitored, a violent eruption on 25 June 1995 claimed the lives of twenty-three people. Only ten of their bodies were recovered. The island's capital Plymouth was covered with ash, then set on fire as lava flows reached the town outskirts.

By 25 August, only 4,000 of the island's original 11,000 inhabitants remained. The rest had been evacuated to Britain or other Caribbean islands. Those who fled received £2,500 compensation from the British government and those who stayed were given aid. Eric Clapton, Paul McCartney, Elton John, Sting and Phil Collins staged at a benefit concert in London for the people of Montserrat.

Apart from the northern tip of the island, Montserrat is now a hell hole of molten lava, ash clouds, noxious gases and rock falls. There is no possibility that the island will ever recover.

The inhabitants should have been warned. Within historical times the island has suffered earthquakes and solfataric vents belched sulphurous gases, thought to relate to intrusions of magma under the Soufrière Hills. Soufrière in French means "sulphur mine".

There are other Soufrière Hills in the Caribbean which had also been active. The Soufrière on Guadeloupe has a history of explosive eruptions that stretch back to the fifteenth century and in 1976 a minor eruption forced the evacuation of thousands of people. And the Soufrière on the island of St Vincent erupted in 1718, 1812 and 1902 – a year which also saw eruptions in Martinique and Guatemala.

The 1718 St Vincent eruption produced lava, which is slow-moving and rarely dangerous, but the eruption in 1812 was explosive and resulted in great loss of life. A new crater 500 feet deep and half a mile wide was formed to the north-east of the original crater and Barbados, some ninety-five miles away, was covered in several inches of ash.

Before the 1812 eruption a conical hill stood in the crater between two lakes, one sulphurous, the other untainted. Its sides were covered with thick vegetation, while white smoke and the occasional blue flame issued from fissures on the peak. For two years there had been seismic activity across the whole region. On 26 March 1812 an earthquake had hit Caracas, killing ten thousand people. The tremor was felt 180 miles away. A month later, on 27 April, the smoke issuing from the top of Soufrière turned black, the earth shook and there was a tremendous noise.

Rocks landed near a boy herding cattle on the slopes. Thinking that other boys were throwing stones at him, he turned to throw them back only to see the volcano was erupting an he ran for his life. Over the next three days and nights the eruption continued until the lava reached the sea.

The eruption ended on 30 April with a loud underground noise. It was over 400 miles away in Caracas and mistaken for cannon fire. Preparations were made to defend the city against invaders. Others reported hearing the noise hundreds of miles in land.

The 1902 eruption on St Vincent occurred at the same time as the eruption of Mount Pelée on Martinque. It began with a series of earthquakes in April. In May, puffs of steam began to emerge from the peak.

On 4 May, the heat on the island became unusually oppressive. People found they could barely breathe. On 5 May the lake in the crater began to boil. Two days later a pyroclastic flow – a mixture of superheated gases and ash – rolled down the mountain killing 1,350 people, though it is said that hundreds escaped death by hiding in a rum cellar. Most of the island's remaining population of Carib Indians were wiped out.

One eyewitness told of his lucky escape: "I was fishing at some distance from the shore when my boatman said to me, 'Look at the Soufrière, sir. It's smoking.' From the top of the cone, reaching far up into the heavens, a dark column of smoke arose, while the mouth of the crater itself glowed like a gigantic forge belching a huge jet of yellow flame. The mass of smoke spread out into branches extending for miles, and clouds of sulphurous vapour, overflowing, as it were, the bowl of the crater, began to roll down the mountain slopes.

"We reached shore and started to run for our lives. We were soon enveloped in impenetrable darkness and I was unable to distinguish the white shirt of my boatman at a yard's distance. But as he knew every inch of the ground, I held on to a stick he had, and so we stumbled on until we reached a place of safety. The incessant roar of the volcano, the rumbling of the thunder, the flashes of the lightning added to the terrific grandeur of the scene. At last we emerged from the pall of death, half suffocated, and with our temples throbbing as if they were going to burst."

More earthquakes followed and six separate streams of lava began pouring down the mountain side. At night the eruption was visible from St Lucia fifty miles away. By 8 May a column of black smoke rose to a height of eight miles. There was loud thunder and spectacular lighting, while the mountain "groaned under the weight of accumulated fury". Rocks and ash fell for miles around. The island was plunged into darkness. A

> **"We reached shore and started to run for our lives."**

black rain began to fall and the air was heavy with the smell of sulphur. A steamer on its way to Kingstown encountered floating ash and pumice, and a cloud of sulphurous gas. When it reached Kingstown – about eight miles from the crater – it found the streets two inches deep in rock and ash. Among the survivors they found there were "many who had been struck by lightning and were paralysed, or who had been scorched by the burning hot sand and were blistered and sore".

By 9 May the showers of rock had stopped but the lava continued to flow. In all, nearly a third of the island was laid waste and 700 feet was lost from the top of the mountain. Hundreds of bodies lay unburied. In one ravine alone eighty-seven were found. They were treated with quicklime, while the carcasses of dead cattle found nearby were burnt.

Another survivor had been rescued with others from a collapsed house.

"We heard the mountain roaring the whole morning," he said, "but we thought it would pass off, and we did not like to abandon our homes, so we chanced it. About half-past one it began to rain pebbles and stones, some of which were alight; but then, although we were afraid, we could not leave. The big explosion must have taken place at half-past two o'clock. There was fire all around me, and I could not breathe. My hands and feet got burned, but I managed to reach the house where the others were. In two hours, everything was over, although pebbles and dust fell for a long time after. My burns got so painful and stiff that I could not move. We remained until Sunday morning without food or water. Five persons died, and as none of us could throw the bodies out, or even move, we had to lie alongside the bodies until we were rescued."

A journalist visiting the region also described the scene: "The entire northern portion of the island is covered with ashes to an average depth of eighteen inches, varying from a thin layer at Kingstown to two feet or more at Georgetown. The crops are ruined, nothing green can be seen, the streets of Georgetown are cumbered with snow-driftlike heaps of ashes, and ashes rest so heavily on the roofs that in several cases they have caused them to fall in. There will soon be 5,000 destitute persons in need of assistance from the government, which is already doing everything possible to relieve the sufferers. There are a hundred injured people in the hospital at Georgetown, gangs of men are searching for the dead or rapidly burying them in trenches, and all that can be done under the circumstances is being accomplished.

"The arrival here of the first detachment of the Ambulance Corps, which brought sufferers from Georgetown caused a sensation. The batch consisted of a hundred persons, whose charred bodies exhaled fetid odours, and whose loathsome faces made even the hospital attendants shudder. All these burned persons were suffering fearfully from thirst and uttering, when strong enough to do so, agonising cries for water. It is doubtful whether any of the whole party will recover.

"While the outbreak of the volcano on the island of Martinique killed more people outright, more territory has been ruined in St Vincent, hence there is greater destitution here. The injured persons are horridly burned by the hot grit, which was driven along with tremendous velocity. Twenty-six persons who sought refuge in a room ten feet by twelve were all killed. One person was brained by a huge stone some nine miles from the crater.

"Rough coffins are being made to receive the bodies of victims. The hospital here is filled with dying people. Fifty injured are lying on the floor of that building, as there are not beds for their accommodation, though cots are being rapidly constructed of boards…

"Since midnight on Tuesday, the subterranean detonations here have ceased, and the Soufrière on Wednesday relapsed, apparently, into perfect repose,

"…we had to lie alongside the bodies until we were rescued."

no smoke rising from the crater, and the fissures emitting no vapour. The stunted vegetation that formerly adorned the slopes of the mountain has disappeared, having given place to grey-coloured lava, which greets the eye on every side. The atmosphere is dry. Rain would be welcome, as there is a great deal of dust in the air, which is disagreeable and irritating to the throats and eyes, and is causing the merchants to put all their dry goods under cover... [Those] who had remained on the estates are half-starved, and the few Carib survivors are leaving their caves and pillaging abandoned dwelling houses and shops...

"The report that the volcanic lake which occupied the top of the mountains has disappeared, now appears to be confirmed. A sea of lava, emitting sulphurous fumes, now apparently occupies the place, and several new craters have been formed. The last time the volcano showed activity, on Tuesday last, the craters, old and new, and numerous fissures in the mountain sides discharged hot vapour, deep subterranean murmurings were heard, the ground trembled at times, from the centre of the volcano huge volumes of steam rose like gigantic pine trees towards the sky, and a dense black smoke, mingling with steam, issued from the new and active crater, forming an immense pall out the northern hills, lowering into the valleys and then rising and spreading until it enveloped the whole island in a peculiar grey mist...

"The sulphurous vapours, which still exhale all over the island, are increasing the sickness and mortality among the surviving inhabitants, and are causing suffering among the new arrivals...

"The stench in the afflicted districts is terrible beyond description. Nearly all the huts left standing are filled with dead bodies. In some cases disinfectants and the usual means of disposing of the dead are useless, and cremation has been resorted to. When it is possible the bodies are dragged with ropes to the trenches and are there hastily covered up,

"The stench in the afflicted districts is terrible beyond description."

quicklime used when available. Many of the dead bodies were so covered with dust that they were not discovered until walked upon by visitors, or by the relieving officers or their assistants...

"The volcano resumed activity on the night of 18 May. Earthquakes were felt on the island, and smoke emanated from fissures and craters on Soufrière. As churchgoers returned from services around 8.30 pm an alarming luminous cloud suddenly ascended many miles high in the north of the island, and drifted sluggishly to the north-east. Incessant lightning fell on the mountain, and one severe flash seemed to strike about three miles from Kingstown. The thunderous rumblings in the crater lasted for two hours and then diminished until they became mere murmurings. During the remainder of the night the volcano was quiet, though ashes fell from ten o'clock until midnight. The inhabitants were frenzied with fear at the time of the outbreak, dreading a repetition of the catastrophe which had caused such terrible loss of life on the island. They ran from the streets into the open country, crying and praying for preservation from another calamity. No one on St Vincent slept that night...

"The continuous agitation of the volcano and the absence of rain caused the vicinity of the afflicted villages to look like portions of the Desert of Sahara. A thick, smoky cloud overspread the island, all business was suspended, the streets were empty and everyone was terror-stricken. The feeling of suspense grew painful. People passed their time gazing at the northern sky, where thunder clouds gathered and the mournful roaring of the volcano was heard. Ashes and pumice fell slowly in the [outlying] districts, and a new reign of terror existed on the island. But during the next day the volcanic disturbances moderated, and some degree of calm returned to the afflicted islanders."

St Vincent did eventually recover from its series of catastrophes, so perhaps there is hope for Montserrat yet.

Sporting Disasters

Investigators sift through the wreckage looking for clues to the cause of the crash

Turin, Italy 1949

On 4 May 1949, the Italian football team Juventus was flying home to Turin after a match in Lisbon. The weather in the Turin area was bad. Visibility at the airport was 1,200 yards with a cloud base of 1,200 feet. But over the 2,200-foot Superga Hill eight miles way, visibility had been reduced by the appalling conditions to just forty yards.

The crew reported into air traffic control as the plane crossed the Italian coast at Savona at 6,000 feet. But then they were forced to descend so they could fly visually. As they began their descent into Turin airport, the aircraft crashed into the church on top of Superga Hill. Along with the crew of four, eighteen players, three executives, two trainers, three journalists and an interpreter died in the crash. An accident investigation ascribed causes of the crash to bad weather, low cloud, poor radio aids and navigation error.

Le Mans, France 1955

Motor racing is a dangerous sport, but usually only for the competitors. The worst disaster in the history of the sport took place on the evening of 11 June 1955. The classic Le Mans 24-Hour race had been underway for almost two-and-a-half hours when the British driving ace Mike Hawthorn in a D-type Jaguar came out of the Arnage hairpin bend and accelerated down the straight towards the White House corner and the pits. Behind him was the famous Argentinian driver Juan Manuel Fangio in a Mercedes.

They were just about to lap another British driver Lance Macklin in a green Austin-Healey and Fangio's team-mate Pierre Levegh. Hawthorn overtook Macklin and pulled over towards the pits

" … kiddies with their heads sliced off. "

which had been calling him in for two laps. As he slowed, Macklin, who was behind him, pulled to his left and began to slide. Levegh and Fangio were fighting for the same stretch of track and Levegh's Mercedes touched Macklin at 180 miles an hour and rammed into the bank, while Fangio masterfully slipped through the gap he had left.

Levegh's car somersaulted. It ploughed through spectators packed at the entrance to a tunnel. Then the fuel tanks exploded and blasted bits of the car into the crowd. Levegh was killed, along with eighty-one spectators.

According to one reporter on the scene: "The engine and back axle of the Mercedes sliced like a razor through the packed spectators. Some were decapitated, and for a hundred yards along the straight the scene was like a bloodstained battlefield. Wailing men and women tried frantically to find out whether their friends or relations were among the

Eighty-one spectators were killed in the crash

Caught on camera: the dramatic moment that Levegh's car somersaulted into the crowd

The race continued despite the accident, eventually being won by Jaguar

victims. Womens' screams rose above the roar of the cars as they continued round the course."

A veteran photographer was also on hand.

"I've covered wars and just about every type of horror job you can think of," he said, "but the stuff I've got here in the can is so appalling that it would make people sick to see it. There are kiddies with their heads sliced off – and their hands still gripping the ice-cream cornets they'd been sucking only seconds before. There was one father, mad with grief, refusing to believe that his son was dead and trying to carry him away to safety."

The bodies were covered with advertising banners that had been torn down. The Mercedes engine, much of it made from the highly flammable metal magnesium, defied firemen and had to be left to burn itself out.

Macklin's car had hit the other bank and came to a halt. He was unhurt. Mercedes pulled out of the race on the instructions of the West German government. But the head of Jaguar, whose

... it would make people sick to see it.

own son had been killed on the way to see the race, insisted that his cars continue. Hawthorn and his co-driver Ivor Bueb went on to win the race.

"It was one time in my career I'd have been equally glad to lose," he said.

Vail, Colorado, USA 1976

In Vail, Colorado in 1976, two gondolas on the ski-lift, each carrying six skiers, crashed 125 feet to the ground. Two young girls and an older woman were killed immediately. Another young man died in hospital in Denver two days later. The other eight people were injured, some severely.

During the accident two gondolas collided, leaving one dangling precariously, held up by a strip of steel just an eighth of an inch thick. And another thirty-nine gondolas, most of them packed to capacity, hung up to 230 feet from the

Thousands flock to ski resorts every year to enjoy the snow

ground. In all 176 people were stranded aloft, wondering when it would be their turn to plummet into the snow below.

There had been warnings that something was wrong. Earlier passengers had reported strange noises coming from the cables and the violent bouncing of the cars. The power had already been shut down, but it was too late. The cable had snapped. The first gondola crashed into a pylon, then fell to the ground. On the way, it hit car 67, knocking it backwards into the oncoming car, number 60. It plummeted to the ground, leaving car 67 damaged and in danger.

The dead and injured were taken from the slopes by toboggan and evacuated by helicopter, but the ski patrols were left with the problem of getting the 176 skiers still marooned in their gondolas down. Fortunately, they were well versed in safety procedures. They climbed up the ski-lift's 135-foot towers, then reached the cars by a specially-modified bicycle that attached to the cable. Once at the gondola, rope was attached to the main cable and the passengers lowered by harness. The process took six hours,

but all the remaining skiers got down safely.

Then, of course, the lawyers moved in, hitting the ski resort and the manufacturers of the ski lift with lawsuits totalling $50 million.

Munich, Germany 1958

On 6 February 1958, Manchester United football team were flying back from Yugoslavia, where they had drawn 3-3 with Red Star Belgrade. On the way, their plane – a twin-engined Elizabethan belonging to British European Airways, now part of British Airways – touched down at Munich Airport to refuel.

The weather conditions there were atrocious. Constant rain turned into snow and, as the plane hit the runway, great plumes of spray spurted over the cabin windows.

An hour later, the plane was ready for

Rescue teams were hindered by the poor weather conditions

takeoff again, but as it roared down the runway its engines did not give it enough power to get off the ground. The aircrew tried again and failed to get off the ground a second time.

The passengers then went back to the departure lounge, while Captain James Thain and his co-pilot Captain Kenneth Rayment discussed what to do with the airport's engineer. He told them that this failure of the "boost surge" necessary for lift-off was common at airports, such as Munich, that were high above sea level. However, they could obtain sufficient power to take off if they opened the throttles more slowly.

Instead of staying in Munich overnight, Captain Thain decided to attempt a third takeoff. Once again the Elizabethan roared down the runway. But it never got airborne. It ran off the end of the runway, across the stopway at the end, through a boundary fence, across a road and into a house where both the house and plane caught fire.

Twenty-three people died. These included United's captain Roger Byne and 21-year-old Duncan Edwards, who was already being hailed as the greatest footballer of his era. Bobby Charlton was injured, but went on to have a distinguished career as a player.

A number of sports journalists accompanying the team also died. This included Frank Swift, who had been an England goalkeeper before turning to journalism.

Captain Kenneth Rayment died, but Captain James Thain survived. He was suspended for thirteen months while a German court of inquiry sat. It decided that the crash had been caused by ice on the wings. Making sure that ice and snow was removed from the wings was considered the pilot's responsibility. Thain insisted that cause of the crash was slush on the runway, which was the responsibility of the airport authorities. He was sacked anyway, but fought on to clear his name.

Captain Thain was sacked by BEA, but fought on to clear his name.

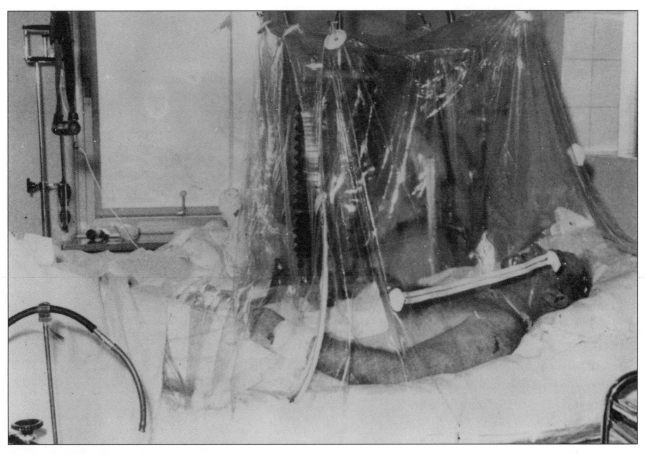

Sir Matt Busby in hospital following the crash

Two years after the disaster, the British Ministry of Aviation published a report saying that an Elizabethan trying to take off in half-an-inch of slush would have needed forty to fifty per cent more runway. The German authorities admitted that there was an inch and a half of slush on the runway at Munich that day. But a second German court of inquiry returned the same verdict. Icing and Thain were to blame.

The British then set up their own court of inquiry and, on 10 June 1969, Thain was exonerated. However, the German authorities refused to re-open their enquiry. James Thain was still fighting for compensation for his dismissal when he died suddenly at the age of fifty-four in 1975.

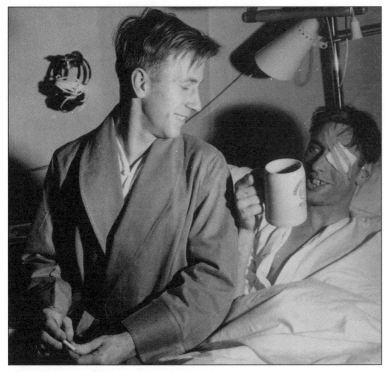

Two of the lucky survivors recovering from their injuries

Lima, Peru 1964

On 24 May 1964, 318 people were killed and another 500 injured in riots at the National Stadium in Lima, Peru after Argentina beat Peru in an Olympic qualifying match. The pandemonium broke out when the referee disallowed a

Peruvian goal in the final two minutes.

Incensed Peru fans spilled out of the stands and broke the stadium windows. Then a crowd of 45,000 went on the rampage in the streets, looting shops, overturning cars and setting buildings on fire. Mounted policemen threw teargas and set dogs on them. Most of the dead were trampled. The government declared a state of emergency and suspended the constitution.

Glasgow, Scotland 1971

Towards the end of the local derby between the two rival football teams Rangers and Celtic in Glasgow, Scotland on 2 January 1971, the score was one nil in Celtic's favour and some of the crowd of 80,000 began to trickle out of the stands at Ibrox Park. Suddenly there was a roar. Rangers had equalised. Fans tried to turn back, meeting others who were now pouring towards the exits.

Crowd pressure built up. On the stairway to Terrace Thirteen the railings burst. Some people were crushed to death against the iron stanchions. Others were suffocated by bodies falling on top of them.

"The bodies just kept pouring on top of one another like water over a waterfall," said one eyewitness.

A policeman was leaving the match when he heard a scream.

"I looked back and saw a pile of bodies about ten feet high," he said, "all laid the same way with their faces towards me – a wall of faces, some with their tongues lolling about."

With other rescuers he tried to give the kiss of life to anyone who showed a faint hope of being revived – usually to no avail. Disentangling the bodies, rescuers came across a number of children – several boys and at least one girl. The bodies were laid out in the gymnasium

The Celtic-Rangers game has always incited passions and guaranteed huge crowds

Sir John Lang and Walter Winterbottom after a meeting with the Minister for Sport in the wake of the crush

under the stand so that relatives could claim them.

"We came away with our boots, socks and the bottoms of our trousers soaked in blood," said the policeman.

Fifty-three died inside the stadium, while another thirteen perished on the way to hospital; the 1–1 draw that day was later stricken from the records.

Moscow, Russia 1982

It seems that 340 soccer fans died in Moscow's Luzhniki Stadium on 20 October 1982, though the Soviet authorities claimed a much lower death toll at the time. In the last minutes of a European Cup match between Soviet club Spartak Moscow and Haarlem of the Netherlands, fans tried to re-enter the stadium after a last-minute goal was scored. Police were blamed for pushing fans back down a narrow, icy staircase

"We came away with our boots, socks and the bottoms of our trousers soaked in blood"

creating a "human mincer".

At the time, the Soviet Sports Committee said only sixty-one died and police did not push fans, while the government newspaper Izvestia put the death toll at sixty-six.

Sheffield, UK 1989

During the 1980s, British soccer was often marred by violence among the fans. On 15 April 1989, a semi-final in the English FA Cup competition was to be played at Hillsborough, Sheffield, between Liverpool FC and Nottingham Forest. Chief Superintendent Duckenfield, who was in charge of policing at the match, told his men that they were to be "firm but fair" – no one was to get in without a ticket, no one was to be let in drunk.

The Liverpool fans had to enter the ground at the Leppings Lane end. But the two turnstiles there could not cope with thousands of fans getting in. Police,

A tribute is lain by a representative of the Players Football Association

Many of the thousands of tributes to the casualties of Hillsborough

fearing fatalities, tried to close perimeter gates so that pressure on the turnstiles could be relieved. It seemed to make things worse. Shortly before kick-off, Chief Superintendent Duckenfield gave orders to open an exit gate. This led straight down a tunnel with a gradient of one in six into a fenced pen of terracing in the lower West Stand which was already completely full. As 2,000 fans rushed down this gradient, many lost their footing and were swept along with their feet completely off the ground. As they crashed into the backs of those already on the terrace, they created a domino effect.

The pressure at the front of the pen became unbearable. People was crushed against crash barriers, unable to escape because of the high metal fences designed to prevent fans invading the pitch.

It soon became clear that something terrible was happening. Six minutes after kick-off, the game was abandoned. Liverpool fans started to climb over the safety fence onto the pitch, where the dying were tended. The police seemed paralysed. Only one ambulance came

... onto the pitch, where the dying were tended.

onto the pitch. Others with highly skilled medical trained personnel remained outside the ground. Ninety-five people died at Hillsborough or in hospital soon after. Another died four years later due to brain damage caused by the disaster.

Chief Superintendent Duckenfield blamed drunken and ticketless Liverpool fans for the disaster. He retired at the age of forty-six on medical grounds. In 1991, a jury returned the verdict of accidental death, but many blame Duckenfield for making the decision to open the exit gate, not blocking the tunnel when the situation got out of hand and not opening the safety gates to allow the fans onto the pitch.

Accra, Ghana 2001

On 9 May 2001, Hearts of Oak and Asante Kotoko, two of the biggest clubs in African football, met at Accra's Sports' Stadium in Ghana. The stadium was packed to capacity, holding 50,000 spectators. Hearts of Oak were the home team, while Kotoko drew its support from the old Ashanti kingdom. They were bitter rivals and fears of trouble meant there was a heavy police presence.

With Hearts of Oak leading 2-1 after two quick goals near the end of the game, Asante Kotoko fans began throwing plastic chairs onto the pitch. Police reacted with teargas. This started a stampede for the exits. A hundred and twenty people were killed in the crush. Fifty more were injured

Harry Zakour, chief executive of Hearts of Oak, criticised police for firing up to a dozen teargas canisters in the stadium when one would have been enough to curb the violence. The government set up an enquiry and declared a period of national mourning.

Hearts of Oak are Accra's local team and have passionate support in the city

Space Disasters

Apollo 1 1967

On 27 January 1967, NASA's Apollo programme that would carry men to the Moon suffered its first casualties. Three astronauts – Virgil I. "Guss" Grisson, Edward H. White and Roger B. Chafee – were burnt to death in the space capsule on the launch pad.

They were on board for a full-scale simulation of the launch, scheduled for 1 February, which was to put them into Earth orbit for fourteen days. The crew had been sealed in the capsule for ten minutes on top of a Saturn V rocket on launch pad 34 at the Kennedy Space Center with no indication of any problem. But then at 6.31 pm the crew reported a fire on board. One of them was heard to say: "Get us out of here."

NASA officials think that an electrical spark started a fire in the pure oxygen atmosphere of the capsule. There were indications that the crew tried to open the hatch. But there were unable to use Apollo's emergency escape system because it was blocked by a gantry.

As rescue teams raced to the scene, the capsule ruptured. Gas and flames burst

"Get us out of here."

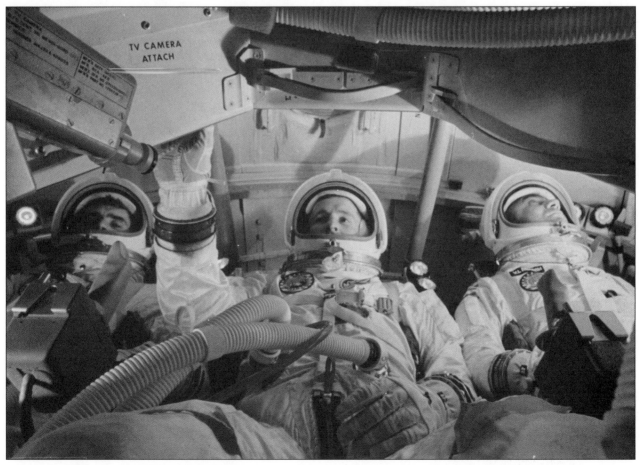

The crew of Apollo 1 await the launch

Apollo 1 in the aftermath of the fire.

Doctors were unable to get to the crew inside the craft and they were eventually removed seven and a half hours after the incident

out of the hole, driving the rescuers back. Thick smoke obscured their vision. Three seconds later there was no further indication of life inside the capsule. Doctors were unable to get to the astronauts and it only proved possible to remove their remains seven-and-a-half hours later.

It was feared that the accident would deal a serious blow to the Apollo programme, which was struggling to stay on schedule after budget cuts. However, the programme resumed in November, when an unmanned Apollo spacecraft went into Earth orbit and on 16 July 1969 Neil Armstrong and Edwin "Buzz" Aldrin became the first men to step on the Moon.

Soyuz 1 1967

At 3.35 am on 23 April 1967 the Soyuz 1 lifted off from the Baykonur Cosmodrome in Kazakhstan. After a full

...no further indication of life...

day in orbit to check the spacecraft's system, the pilot Vladimir Komarov was due to be joined in orbit by Soyuz 2 carrying a crew of three. The spacecrafts were then to dock and two of the crew members of Soyuz 2 were to spacewalk to Soyuz 1.

Soyuz 1 reached orbit without any problem. But then things began to go wrong. The left solar panel failed to deploy, leaving the craft with only half the electrical power needed. Only the backup communications system worked and it proved impossible to manoeuvre the craft.

By the fifth orbit Soyuz 1 was out of control. The launch of Soyuz 2 was cancelled and it was decided to bring Komarov home. But between the seventh and thirteenth orbits, he was out of radio range.

After the thirteenth orbit, mission control instructed Komarov to fire the retro-rockets on the seventeenth orbit. The de-orbit burn was successful and the drogue chute opened. But a pressure sensor failed and the main chute would

Leonid Brezhnev was the first to be informed of the perilous situation of Soyuz 1

not deploy. Komarov released the reserve chute, but this became tangled with the drogue chute and did nothing to slow the spacecraft. It crashed into a field in Orenburg, southern Russia, at 7 am on 24 April at over 300 miles an hour.

Komarov survived the re-entry but not the terrible impact with the ground. The retro-rockets exploded on impact and a fire engulfed what remained of the Soyuz descent module.

In the Soviet Union, bad news was suppressed, so the local air force commander reported to the control centre only that the cosmonaut would require immediate medical attention, then severed all communication links. The Soviet premier Leonid Brezhnev was informed of the real situation at midday and the Soviet newsagency TASS announced Komarov's death seven hours later.

...later found more of Komarov's remains

Among those who worked at US listening posts in Turkey the story circulated that Komarov was infuriated by the bulky Soviet spacecraft and died cursing those who had sent him into space in such decrepit craft.

His ashes were buried in the wall of the Kremlin in a huge ceremony. However, it is said that a group of Young Pioneers later found more of Komarov's remains at the crash site and gave him a second burial.

Soyuz 11 1971

On 6 June 1971, Georgy Dobrovolsky, Viktor Patsayev and Vladislav Volkov blasted off in their Soviet Soyuz 11 spacecraft. The following day they docked with the Salyut 1 space station and crawled through into the forty-six-foot-long orbiting laboratory. They were its first crew and conducted the first scientific experiments and observations on board.

They stayed there for twenty-four days, the longest anyone had stayed in weightless space at that time. Then they crawled back into Soyuz 11, undocked and headed back to Earth. Re-entry

Georgy Dobrovolsky

Viktor Patsayev

...a fatal rise in their blood pressure.

any physical injuries. A post-mortem revealed that the three cosmonauts were killed by a fatal rise in their blood pressure. Air had escaped through a hole created in the door seal when the landing capsule separated from the main craft and the cabin had become depressurised.

The three men were named Heroes of the Soviet Union and buried in the Kremlin wall alongside the first man in space Yuri Gagarin, who had died in a plane crash in 1968.

went perfectly and the spacecraft made a soft landing in Kazakhstan on 29 June. But when the recovery teams opened the hatch, they found the crew inside dead.

They did not appear to have suffered

Vostok Rocket 1980

On 18 March 1980, an accident occurred during the launch of a Vostok rocket at the Plesetsk cosmodrome in north-west Russia. The explosion of three hundred tons of fuel completely

All three cosmonauts were buried in the Kremlin wall alongside Yuri Gagarin

destroyed the launch pad and incinerated its surroundings, leaving forty-eight dead. Doctors at a nearby hospital said injured personnel suffered acute burns, in particular to their lungs.

The rocket had been carrying a military spy satellite, Ikar, and *Pravda*, the Soviet Communist Party paper, reported that the launch had been a success.

A state commission which investigated the tragedy at the time concluded that operator error was to blame for the accident. It said the blast had been caused by the escape of liquid oxygen. But twenty years after the event, the Russian TV station NTV International revealed the truth. Its programme, called Independent Investigation, established that the launch-pad explosion been caused by oxygen peroxide leaking from the rocket due to the poor quality of its fuel filters.

The programme also said that the pre-launch procedures at the Plesetsk cosmodrome have not been changed since the blast and that the launch pad has never been modernised since it was built.

"The design centre drafted the blueprints for the facility during the Cold War and the safety of personnel was the least of its worries," it said.

Challenger 1986

At 11.38 am on 28 January 1986, the Space Shuttle Challenger lifted off from its launch pad at Cape Canaveral on a routine mission. Just 0.678 seconds into the flight, a puff of grey smoke appeared from a joint on the right Solid Rocket Booster.

Mission control at Houston

"Roger, go for full power."

Challenger landing
after yet another
routine mission

Eight more puffs of increasingly blacker smoke appeared between 0.836 and 2.500 seconds as the rubber O-rings in the joint seal were being burned and eroded by the hot propellant gases.

Both the Shuttle's main engines and the Solid Rockets Boosters operated at reduced thrust until the Shuttle passed through the area of maximum dynamic pressure, before throttling up to escape the Earth's gravity. The last words from the shuttle were: "Go for full power."

Then the main engines was throttled up to 104 per cent thrust. At the same time, the Solid Rocket Boosters were increasing their thrust when the first flickering flame appeared on the right Solid Rocket Booster in the area of the defective joint.

It first appeared at 58.788 seconds into the flight. By 59.262 seconds, it had grown into a well-defined plume. This was directed onto the Shuttle's external tank which contained an explosive mixture of over 385,000 gallons of liquid hydrogen and 140,000 gallons of liquid oxygen. It burnt through the metal skin of the tank and, at 64.660 seconds, there was an abrupt change in the shape and colour of the plume.

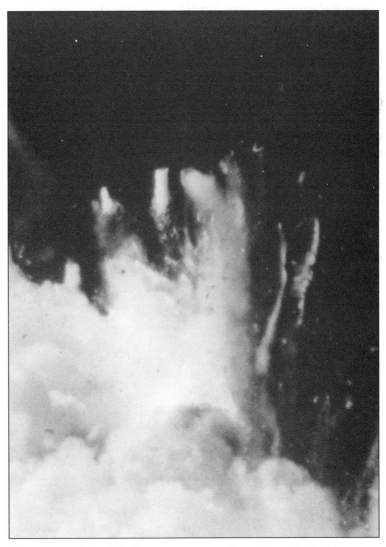

The moment the Challenger was enveloped in a fireball

Debris continued to rain down to earth more than an hour after the explosion

The Challenger crew, including high school teacher Christa McAuliffe

At about 72.20 seconds, the lower strut of the Solid Rocket Booster broke free from the weakened hydrogen tank. This meant the Shuttle could no longer be controlled.

At 73.124 seconds, white vapour pattern bloomed from the side of the External Tank. This indicated the catastrophic structural failure of the hydrogen tank, releasing massive amounts of liquid hydrogen which created a sudden forward thrust of about 2.8 million pounds. The freely flapping Solid Rocket Booster then smashed into the liquid oxygen tank, which failed at 73.137 seconds. Within milliseconds the escaping oxygen mixed with the hydrogen causing a massive, almost explosive, burning.

Travelling at Mach 1.92 at a height of 46,000 feet – over eight miles – the Challenger was totally enveloped in a fireball. The Orbiter broke into several large sections which emerged from the fireball. One of them was the forward fuselage carrying the crew. All seven were killed. They were the commander, Francis R. Scobee; the pilot, Michael J. Smith; and astronauts Judith A. Resnik, Ronald E. McNair, Ellison S. Onizuka, Gregory B. Javis and Christa McAuliffe, a high school teacher from Concord, New Hampshire, who had been chosen from thousands of applicants to be the first ordinary citizen to go into space. Her pupils were among those watching the launch on TV that day.

In the crowd at Cape Canaveral were Mrs McAuliffe's husband, her two children and her parents. Cheers gave way to a stunned silence as two huge white streamers emerged from the fireball and debris began to rain down over the ocean. This continued for more than an hour afterwards. For weeks a flotilla of space agency and Coast Guard

No signs of the crew were found.

craft scoured the crash site, some twenty miles out to sea. No signs of the crew were found.

The cause of the explosion was found to be an O-ring failure in the right Solid Rocket Booster. Cold weather the night before the launch had made it brittle, stopping it sealing the joint between the sections of the booster properly.

Columbia 2003

At about 9 am Eastern Standard Time on 1 February 2003, NASA's Mission Control at Houston, Texas lost radio contact with the space shuttle Columbia as it descended from orbit towards Cape Canaveral in Florida. The shuttle was flying at about 203,000 feet – thirty-eight miles – and just re-entering the Earth's atmosphere. Travelling at over 12,500 miles an hour or Mach 18, it broke up over north central Texas.

NASA had already had indications that something was wrong. Temperature sensors and hydraulic systems on the left wing had failed. Seconds later indicators showed a loss of tyre pressure on the left landing gear and there were indications of excessive heating. At about 5.54 am Pacific Standard Time – 8.54 am Eastern Standard Time – a California news photographer observed pieces breaking away from the Shuttle as it passed overhead and a red flare coming from the Shuttle itself.

At about 9.05 am EST, residents of north central Texas reported a loud boom. Video footage shot at Dallas, Texas showed two, then multiple contrails and flaming debris falling from the sky. Soon debris began raining down from the clear skies above the counties south-east of Dallas. This continued for several minutes. Pieces of wreckage and human remains were found as far away as western Louisiana and the south-western counties of Arkansas. Some caused some damage and started grass

Columbia had already completed a number of missions without incident

It is thought a piece of insulation fell off an external fuel tank during takeoff, damaging the Columbia's left wing

fires. No-one was hit, but dozens of people were admitted to hospital after being burnt by handling hot pieces of wreckage.

The accident seems to have been caused by a piece of insulation which had fallen off the external fuel tank on take-off. It appeared to hit the Shuttle's left wing. Reviewing video footage of the take-off the following day, NASA concluded that the "event did not present a safety concern". It was later thought that the foam had dislodged some of the ceramic tiles that protect the underside of the Shuttle's wing from overheating during re-entry.

All seven of the Columbia's crew were lost. They were the commander, Rick Husband; the pilot, William McCool; and astronauts Michael Anderson, David Brown, Kalpana Chawla, Laurel Clark and Ilan Ramon, the first Israeli to go into space. His presence on the mission led to speculation that Columbia had been the victim of a terrorist attack, which was later dismissed.

"...did not present a safety concern"

Avalanches

It is believed that Hannibal lost over half his Carthaginian army to avalanches as he trekked across the Alps

...he lost between 18,000 and 30,000 troops

Italian Alps 218 BC

When Hannibal crossed the Alps in the autumn of 218 BC, it is estimated that he lost between 18,000 and 30,000 troops – something approaching half of his Carthaginian army – to avalanches, along with much of his baggage train and some of his thirty-eight elephants. The journey took fifteen days. Some of the avalanches may have been started deliberately by Alpine tribesmen hindering his march on Italy.

Avalanches can be sudden, and their power devastating. 96 people lost their lives in the Stevens Pass

Cascade Mountains, USA 1910

On 1 March 1910 two Great Northern Railway trains were halted by heavy snow at Stevens Pass in the Cascade Mountains, north-east of Seattle, Washington. One train was a local passenger train; the other was a fast mail from the east. They had arrived a few days before at Wellington, just on the west side of the pass. All the efforts of the railroad company to get them safely across the pass and off the mountain had failed.

Snow was falling at a rate of a foot an hour and the railroad's snow ploughs were out of coal. Food supplies were getting low and a tremendous lightning storm had been raging for hours. Hundreds of feet above the railroad tracks an ice shelf broke loose, sending tons of snow, slush and ice hurtling downhill, sweeping along with it trees and rocks. In the small hours of the morning, the avalanche struck the trains.

The force of the sliding snow pushed both trains into the Tye river valley, 150 feet below, then swept them on for another 300 yards. The cars were crushed and the remains were buried under forty feet of snow and debris. Ninety-six people lost their lives in the avalanche, making this the worst train disaster in American history.

Peru 1962

In 1962 in Peru some 4,000 people were killed by an extinct volcano called Mount Huascarah. The summer started late that year and the people of the small village of Ranrahirca, two hundred miles north-west of the capital Lima, were out sunning themselves when the hot summer sun began melting part of the icecap. It broke off, starting an avalanche of snow, water, mud and rock.

The landslide hit the village at seven pm, when most people were indoors. It swept over the church, the school, the village halls and all the houses, coming to rest on the banks of the Santa river. In just eight minutes 450 of Ranrahirca's 500 residents were dead, buried under forty feet of debris. But Ranrahirca was not the only place that was hit. At least three other villages were destroyed and it is estimated that 4,000 died in all in outlying hamlets and remote ranches.

The landslide was three-quarters of a mile wide. It brought down telephone lines and news of the tragedy did not reach Lima for many hours.

Train Crashes

The Tay Bridge disaster was the worst failure of structural engineering in the British Isles

The salvage operation recovered no survivors

Tay Bridge, Scotland 1879

The first Tay railway bridge was opened on 31 May 1878. Designed by Thomas Bouch, the Tay Bridge was nearly two miles long – the longest bridge in the world at the time. Its eighty-five spans supported on thin cast-iron columns carried a single rail track. The track ran on top of seventy-two of these spans. But in the central thirteen spans, the track ran through a boxed lattice of girders. These so-called "high girders" had sides twenty-seven feet tall and stood eighty-eight feet above the high water mark.

At 7.13 pm on Sunday the 28 December 1879, a train carrying seventy-five passengers left St. Fort travelling towards Dundee and steamed onto the bridge. It was a stormy night with winds of almost hurricane strength, gusting up to eighty miles an hour. With the train on the bridge, the structure began to weaken and the central girders gave way. Eye witnesses described sparks flying out of the engine as the train and its six carriages plunged into the river. All on board died. It was the worst failure of structural engineering in the history of the British Isles.

A Court of Inquiry concluded that "the fall of the bridge was occasioned by the insufficiency of the cross bracing and its fastenings to sustain the force of the gale" and Sir Thomas Bouch – he had been knighted by Queen Victoria after completing the bridge – was blamed. While it seems clear that Bouch had not allowed sufficiently for wind loading, it is unlikely that the design of the bridge could have withstood the winds that night even had it been reinforced.

The locomotive from the crash was recovered, and renamed, with grim humour, 'The Diver'. The flat deck girders, all of which remained standing after the disaster, were re-used in the present bridge and are still in use today.

Many of India's trains are dangerously overcrowded and in need of updating

Samastipur, India 1981

The worst train disaster in history occurred on 6 June 1981 when an overcrowded train plunged off a bridge at Samastipur, north India, into the Bagmati River. Around 900 people were killed. The driver had braked suddenly to avoid a cow. A cyclone in the area may also have been a factor.

Seven carriages fell from the bridge and were swept away. The number of casualties had been swelled by the fact that there were several large wedding parties on board. Hundreds of people were travelling on the roof and the footboards. Navy divers had to use underwater explosives to blow off the doors. They were called in after local divers had refused to touch the train because of the hundreds of bodies trapped inside. Local boatmen refused the $5 reward for each body recovered.

Tangiwai Bridge, New Zealand 1953

On Christmas Eve 1953, a young postal worker named Cyril Ellis was driving home to Taihape in New Zealand. His route took him over the bridge at Tangiwai which crossed the normally placid Whangaehu river.

The river was fed by a warm volcanic lake whose outflow ran through a tunnel beneath the Whangaehu Glacier. But the tunnel had been blocked by volcanic activity a couple of years before and the water in the lake rose to twenty-six feet above normal. The warm water melted the glacier and suddenly the whole thing gave way.

That night, instead of a trickling stream, Ellis saw ahead of him a raging torrent. Carrying with it chunks of ice and boulders, it had washed away the bridge that carried both the road and the main railway line. Ellis looked at his watch. It was 10.20 pm. He knew that the Wellington to Auckland express was due. That night the train was packed with holidaymakers on their way to Auckland where the newly crowned Queen Elizabeth II was to make a speech the next day.

Ellis ran up the line tried to signal to the train to stop with his flashlight. He saw the driver standing on the footplate as the train raced past. Somehow the driver managed to pull on the brake. But there was no way it could pull up in time. The engine and the first five passenger cars plunged into the abyss. Three remained behind on the track, while another hung at a precarious 45° angle. Ellis was trying to help those aboard get out, when the carriage crashed into the river beneath and began filling with water. He smashed the window and managed to rescue all but one of the twenty-two passengers. One young girl had drowned beneath a seat before he could get to her.

Another twenty-eight managed to escape from the forward cars, including an elderly woman found 300 yards downstream. Of the 285 passengers on board, 151 were killed and twenty were never accounted for.

Cyril Ellis and a passenger named John Holman were awarded the George

The driver applied the brakes, but nothing happened

Medal for their bravery in rescuing trapped souls that night. Another passing motorist, Arthur Bell, and train guard William Inglis were awarded the British Empire Medal.

Blue Mountain Express, Sydney 1977

On 18 January 1977, the Blue Mountain express, filled with commuters heading for their workplaces in Sydney, was running several minutes late. In order to avoid becoming held up behind a slow commuter train, the express was travelling at the maximum speed permitted on the line, 80km/h. Although the train began to slow for a temporary speed restriction, imposed on a section of track where maintenance was being carried out, it seems that it was still travelling too fast. As the train took a bend, the locomotive derailed. It then careered along the rails for 50 metres before crashing into the Bold Street Bridge, which spanned the railway line. The locomotive, with the first two carriages still attached, smashed the bridge stanchions before coming to a rest further down the line.

The full weight of the now unsupported road bridge collapsed onto carriages three and four, and this is where the death toll mounted; forty-four passengers in carriage three, and thirty-one in carriage four were crushed instantly, with more fatalities caused by cars falling from the road above.

The situation was complicated by the huge section of road balanced on carriage three, too heavy to be lifted by any cranes that were available. As rescuers worked frantically to free those survivors trapped inside the wrecked carriages, LPG bottles, used as fuel for the carriage heating ruptured, adding further danger to survivors and rescuers alike. One man was about to start a chainsaw inside the carriage until he realised the danger, and started it outside.

The death toll eventually reached 83, with over 200 injured, many seriously.

The official enquiry into the disaster exonerated the train crew, laying the blame on poor maintenance of the tracks.

Mont Cenis, France 1917

Near midnight of 12 December 1917, a troop train laden with French soldiers climbed through the Mont Cenis rail tunnel high in the French Alps. It then began the steep descent to the town of Modane in the valley of the Maurienne and the heavy train rapidly began gathering speed.

The driver applied the brakes, but nothing happened. The train was loaded well beyond the safety limits, making it up to four times too heavy for the brakes on the locomotive or the first carriages. The brakes were soon glowing white hot, sparking fires in the carriagesThe train derailed at break-neck speed, killing up to 800 men. Four hundred and twenty-four were identified by their dog-tags. Sometimes that was all that could be found of them. The remaining 135 were buried in a communal grave. The death toll from this crash makes it the worst rail disaster ever.

As World War I was underway, the news was censored to avoid giving comfort to the enemy and, set against the carnage of the Western Front, the loss of life seemed small beer – except to the families of the dead. The records kept by the French War Office and French Railways were destroyed in World War II.

The Mont Cenis tunnel was an incredible feat of 19th century engineering

Fires

London 1666

The Great Fire of London of 1666 destroyed the medieval capital of England. An area half a mile by one-and-a-half miles – 373 acres within the city wall and sixty-three acres outside it – was completely destroyed. The old St Paul's Cathedral, most of the municipal buildings, the halls of the forty-four livery companies, eighty-seven churches and 13,200 houses were burnt down. But amazingly only six people are known to have died. Indeed the fire might even have saved lives as it killed the rats that had brought the plague to the city the year before, killing over 70,000.

The fire began at the bakery of Thomas Farynor in Pudding Lane near London Bridge on 2 September 1666. At 2 am Farynor's assistant awoke to find the house full of smoke. He woke his master who slept in the apartment above the shop and they climbed out of the window, along some guttering and escaped through the house next door. But Farynor's maid was too frightened to make the climb and became the fire's first victim.

Sparks from the burning bakery fell on hay in the yard of the Star Inn in Fish Street Hill. Flames from the blazing inn set fire to St Margaret's church. The fire quickly consumed the buildings of Pudding Lane and Fish Street Hill and spread down to the riverside wharves where coal, timber and hay lay on the open quays. The warehouses nearby were packed with hemp, oil, tallow, spirits and other highly flammable materials.

Soon the flames were halfway across the old London Bridge and only a break caused by a fire in 1633 prevented the fire from spreading across to Southwark on the south side of the river.

The celebrated diarist Samuel Pepys awoke at 7 am in his house in Seething Lane to find that more than three hundred houses, along with the Fishmonger's Hall, were on fire and a stiff breeze was fanning the flames. He rushed to Whitehall to warn the court.

There was little that could be done to fight the fire. Although each city parish was obliged to provide buckets, ladder, axes and fire hooks, the equipment was poorly maintained. The only water had

373 acres of London were completely destroyed by the raging inferno

to be carried by hand from the Thames. The waterwheels under the arches of London Bridge which powered the water supply had already been destroyed. When it was suggested that houses should be pulled down to create a fire break, the Lord Mayor of London wanted to know who was going to pay for the damage. Eventually, he gave his permission for houses to be pulled down, provided the owner gave his permission.

Pepys returned from Whitehall with orders from Charles II to pull down the houses, but the owners argued, often delaying the demolition until the building was on fire, which meant it was not effective as a fire break. Despite the efforts of the authorities, the following day began with one-sixteenth of the city ablaze. By the end of the day, a quarter of the city had been burnt out. The Royal Exchange, the Old Bailey and the Guildhall were destroyed – though, fortunately, the city's records, which were kept in the Guildhall's crypt, were saved.

On the third day, gunpowder was used to create firebreaks, but a lot of property was destroyed unnecessarily. The Boar's Head, a tavern in Eastcheap favoured by Shakespeare and Ben Johnson, was burned down. But the old St Paul's Cathedral, which was built of stone with a lead roof and protected by a broad churchyard, was thought to be fireproof. But the wind carried a cinder up onto the roof. This caught some boards used to patch a leak. From there the fire spread to the beams. Molten lead dripped from the roof and the stones of the walls exploded like grenades.

Inside the vaulted basement of St Paul's was St Faith's, the church of the booksellers' guild where £200,000 worth of books were stored. Among them was an entire Third Folio edition of Shakespeare's plays, which was destroyed.

Eventually the wind dropped and the fire was brought under control. By then eighty per cent of the city was in ashes. Between 100,000 and 200,000 people were homeless. At the time, Britain was at war with France and Holland. There

A monument stands in London to this day commemorating the great fire of 1666

were rumours that the fire had been started by enemy agents. A crazed French watchmaker named Robert Hubert confessed. He was hanged. It has subsequently been proved that he landed in England two days after the fire started.

Within days, the architect Christopher Wren submitted a great plan to rebuild the city with a new regularised street plan. It was rejected. Instead, the city was rebuilt along the old street plan to preserve the rights of those who owned property. But Wren did get to build the new St Paul's and many other new churches in the city. The new houses were built in brick and stone, instead of wood. There were strict building codes and a Fire Company was founded in

Farynor's maid was too frightened to make the jump, and became the fire's first victim

1667. This ran a private fire brigade which protected buildings that were insured with the company.

The Monument in London, a two-hundred-foot column completed in 1677, commemorates the place where the Great Fire of London started. Originally it bore an inscription blaming the fire on a Catholic conspiracy. This has since been removed.

Chicago, 1871

In 1871, Chicago was just forty years old. Though it appeared to have many stone buildings, most merely had a stone façade. An estimated sixty-five per cent of the city's 60,000 buildings were made from timber.

Added to that there were fifty-five miles of pine-block streets and 651 miles of wooden sidewalks. Even the newly opened Union Stockyards were paved with wood to protect the hooves of the livestock on their way to the slaughter houses.

The bridges over the Chicago river were made of wood, as were the ships moored there. Wood shavings and kindling for starting fires were kept in wood sheds or under wooden houses. In short the city was a fire trap, especially in the summer of 1871. There had been a drought – the worst in living memory – across the Great Plains and Chicago was tinder dry.

Fires had broken out in the city all summer long. By the first week of October, the five-ton bell on the Cook County Courthouse was sounding the fire alarm as many as seven times a day.

Then on the night of Saturday 7 October one of the worst fires in the history of Chicago broke out. A lumber mill on Canal Street went up. Four square blocks on the West Side were burnt out. The sixteen-hour battle against the flames left the city's fire department exhausted. According to one

General Sheridan was called in to impose martial law in the wake of the fire

report, after they had finally got the fire under control, they had done a little too much celebrating.

Engine Company Number Six had returned to Canal Street at about 8 pm on 8 October. Forty-five minutes later, a resident of DeKoven Street named Dennis Kogan spotted flames coming out of the barn behind the framed house at 137, which belonged to Mr and Mrs Patrick O'Leary. He woke them. Another neighbour, William Lee, rushed to call the fire department at around 9 pm but, for some reason, the call did not register on the city's telegraphic system. However, a lookout on the cupola of the courthouse spotted it, but mistook the location. At 9.20 pm the lookout on the tower of Engine Company Number Six also spotted the fire. The alarm was sounded and the company reached DeKoven Street at about 9.24 pm. The fire had already taken hold and was being fanned by the breeze. Ten minutes later, Engine Company Number Five turned up, but incredibly, all their equipment failed.

By 10 pm sparks had caught fire to the steeple of St Paul's Church five blocks north. Then the fire caught the furniture factory next door. By 11 pm, burning debris was falling two miles out in Lake Michigan. And by 11.30 pm, aided by a sixty-mile-an-hour wind, the fire had jumped the south branch of the Chicago River into the South Side.

It levelled the red-light district of Conley's Patch in a matter of minutes. The "fireproof" *Chicago Tribune* building was razed, along with the mayor's office, the fire department and the courthouse, sending the five-ton bell crashing into the basement.

they were cushioned by the bodies of those who had fallen before them

Chicagoans still hoped that the main branch of the Chicago river would prevent the fire spreading to the North Side. It didn't. Burning debris was carried over the river on the wind and set fire to the waterworks. By 3 am on Monday morning, the pumps were out of action. Firefighters had come from as far away as Cincinnati and Milwaukee but, without water, there was nothing they could do to stop the flames. However, by 11 pm the fire burnt itself out.

Some three hundred people were killed – the death toll is not known precisely as some corpses would have been incinerated completely in temperatures that rose to 1600°C in places. Some drowned as they tried to swim out to boats in the lake which, in turn, caught fire. One man buried his wife and children in the sand, leaving air holes of them to breathe facing away from the fire. He waded out into the lake and stood up to his neck in water for seven hours under he was rescued by a passing tug.

Nearly 18,000 buildings covering 2,124 acres had been burnt out, causing an estimated $196 million of damage, and General Sheridan, famed from the Civil War, was called in to impose martial law.

According to the *Chicago Evening Journal*: "All the principal hotels, all the

Chicago was growing rapidly in the early 1900s, and many buildings did not meet basic safety standards

public buildings, all the banks, all the newspaper offices, all the places of amusement, nearly all the great business edifices, nearly all the railroad depots, the water works, the gas works, several churches, and thousands of private residences and stores have been consumed. The proud, noble, magnificent Chicago of yesterday is today a mere shadow of what it was."

But Chicago was soon open for business again. In a maelstrom of philanthropy, the city was reconstructed. Queen Victoria, Alfred Lord Tennyson, Thomas Carlyle and John Ruskin all sent books to restock the libraries. In six weeks, 212 stone and brick buildings were under construction on the South Side. With a year, $40 million of buildings had been erected − finer than those they replaced − and by 1880 the scar on the fabric of the city had completely healed.

That only left the question: who was to blame? The story that Mrs O'Leary's cow had kicked over a kerosene lamp while being milked soon spread. Mrs O'Leary claimed that she, her husband and their five children were all in bed when the fire started. Nevertheless an angry mob believed that her husband was responsible and aimed to lynch him. The O'Learys hid in the attic of their house which − ironically − had escaped the flames. Patrick O'Leary eventually escaped the city in disguise.

Another suspect was the O'Learys' lodger, a one-legged dray-man named Dennis "Peg Leg" Sullivan. It seems he had been drinking secretly in the barn, possibly with Dennis Kogan, the man who had sounded the alarm − because Mrs O'Leary did not approve − and set fire to the hay with his pipe. He claimed that he had seen the flames from across the street and rushed to the barn to rescue the livestock, losing his wooden leg on the way. His affidavit insisting that he was not responsible was duly signed with an X.

Chicago 1903

In December 1903, a troupe of actors from Drury Lane, London, came to

An estimated 65 per cent of Chicago's buildings and structures were made from timber

That only left the question: who was to blame?

Chicago to perform a traditional English pantomime at the Iroquois Theatre in Chicago.

It was called Mr Bluebeard and a cut-price matinee drew a record crowd of over 1,700 on the afternoon of 30 December. At 3.15 pm, the performance was in full swing. There were around 400 actors and stagehands backstage. The performers onstage were singing "In the Pale Moonlight". The moonlight effect was produced by shining a bright-blue arc-light through gauze. It seems that one of these lights overheated, setting the gauze on fire. The stagehands tried to put it out, but there were no proper fire extinguishers backstage. Soon the scenery – made from highly flammable canvas painted with oil – caught fire. Someone shouted "Fire!" and the audience began to panic.

The stagehands dropped the asbestos safety curtain, but it snagged on a wire. The flames shot out into the auditorium under it, fanned by the draft coming through a stage door left open by the fleeing company.

There was a stampede for the exits. There were thirty fire exits, but they were poorly marked. The aisles were too narrow to handle the crowd and on the landings the exit gates were locked to prevent people from the balcony moving to the more expensive seats in the circle.

The audience ran out onto the fire escapes that ran down the back of the building. But these were inadequate. Flames from below made some impassable. People were killed in the crush. Some fell or jumped over the sides. A few survived the fall, but only because they were cushioned by the bodies of those who had fallen before them. Twelve people escaped by crawling along planks pushed across the narrow alleyway at the back of the theatre from the buildings behind. Others perished waiting their turn.

The Drury Lane Players were used to more salubrious surroundings

Immigrants pouring into Ellis Island, soon found themselves in poorly run factories earning minimum wages

When the fire department arrived, they quickly doused the flames. The death toll was 602. Some 200 had died from the effects of flames and smoke from the fire which had lasted just ten minutes. The rest had been crushed or trampled to death. There were the marks of boots and shoes on the faces of the dead and, in places, the flesh had been trampled from the bones.

It was discovered that no fire drill had ever been held in the theatre and inspectors had been bought off with free tickets. Within days, there was a nation-wide inspection of theatres. Fifty were closed as fire hazards and new fire regulations for places of public entertainment were introduced.

Triangle Shirtwaist Factory, New York 1911

At around 4.45 pm on 25 March 1911, a fire broke out in a bin of fabric remnants on the eight floor of the Asch building on the corner of Washington Place and Greene Street in New York City. This was part of a sweatshop called the Triangle Shirtwaist Factory that occupied the eighth, ninth and tenth floors of the building. It employed a large workforce of largely immigrant women, who worked long hours in unsanitary conditions in a factory that paid little heed to building and safety codes.

The fire services were ill-equipped to deal with fast-spreading fires

The firm's production manager tried to douse the flames, but the fire hose was rotten and but there was no water. As the flames spread, panic broke out. Women raced down the stairs. The workers on the tenth floor were warned by telephone. They joined the headlong crush down the stairs or ran up the stairs to the roof.

Flames erupted on the ninth floor without warning. Some 250 dashed for the single door that led to the stairwell – only to find it locked. Some women crammed themselves into the elevator. Others threw themselves on the roof of the descending car, only to have more women fall on top of them.

By the time the fire department arrived, women were already throwing themselves out of the windows. The firemen's ladders only reached to the sixth floor and the water from their hoses could not reach the figures seen smouldering on the window ledges above.

Some women made their way to the fire escape at the back of the building. But that did not reach all the way down to the ground, stopping at the second storey. Those in the front were forced off the bottom of the fire escape by the weight of those behind. The heat then began to melt the fire escape. Its bolts then began to pop and the whole thing finally collapsed.

Women were still jumping from the upper floors. The firemen tried to catch them, but the falling women went right through the nets they stretched out. Eventually the piles of bodies became so heavy that it restricted the flow of water through the hoses.

...women were already throwing themselves out of the windows

The area around the Lagos armoury was densely populated

Many of the women who died had gone on strike the year before, complaining of the safety conditions. The Triangle Shirtwaist Factory disaster resulted in stricter safety codes and fire-fighting equipment became mandatory on all commercial premises.

Lagos, Nigeria 2002

On 27 January 2002, an explosion in an armoury rocked Lagos, leaving as many as 2,000 dead. After the initial explosion on the night of the 27th, multiple secondary explosions occurred into the morning of the 28th with shells and flaming debris raining down on the city for miles around. Shock waves shattered windows six miles from the scene. Hundreds died when they fled and fell into the weed-choked Oke Afa canal, where they drowned. Not realising how deep the canal was, some people drove their vehicles into it.

Bomb disposal experts then had the task of defusing some two hundred live warheads within the compound and another five hundred outside it in the adjoining neighbourhoods.

The armoury was old and had been built when the area was not populated. Many Nigerians thought it should have been moved long before. The state governor of, Lagos Bola Ahmed Tinubu, accused the army of negligence and Nigeria's two houses of parliament announced inquiries into the blast.